Learning Resources Centre

Kingston College
Kingston Hall Road
Kingston upon Thames
KT1 2AQ

A *Letts*

e Guide

First published 1994
Reprinted 1998
This edition revised by Ron Simpson

Letts Educational
Aldine House
Aldine Place
London W12 8AW
0181 740 2266

Text © John Mahoney and Stewart Martin 1994

Self-test questions devised by Sandra Lissenden

Typeset by Jordan Publishing Design

Text design Jonathan Barnard

Text illustrations Hugh Marshall

Cover illustration Ivan Allen

Design © BPP (Letts Educational) Ltd

Acknowledgements
Outline answers are solely the responsibility of the author, and are not supplied
or approved by the Exam Board.

British Library Cataloguing in Publication Data
A CIP record for this book is available from the British Library

ISBN 1 85758 256 X

Printed and bound in Great Britain

Ashford Colour Press, Gosport, Hampshire

Letts Educational is the trading name of BPP (Letts Educational) Ltd

Contents

■ Plot synopsis

Set in the 1840s, the novel tells the story of Bathsheba Everdene and the three men who feature in her life.

Gabriel Oak is the first to propose to Bathsheba. He has a small sheep farm, having previously worked as a shepherd and as a bailiff. She declines his offer and then, for a time, disappears from his life when she inherits a farm from her uncle. Fate intervenes when Gabriel's flock is lost and he has to look for work. Passing by a farm near Weatherbury, he sees the ricks on fire and leads the successful attempt to save them. He discovers it is Bathsheba's farm and he is given work by her.

Bathsheba sends a valentine to a local farmer, Mr Boldwood. She does it lightheartedly, but the consequences are dire. Boldwood develops an unbalanced passion for her. Bathsheba is unable to cope with his demands: whilst she does not love him or want to marry him, she seems incapable of giving him a clear refusal.

Sergeant Troy, a dashing soldier, casts a spell over Bathsheba. Infatuated, she marries him. The marriage destroys Boldwood and saddens Gabriel. Troy is not a farmer and his thoughtless actions put the ricks in danger – yet again Gabriel comes to the rescue. Troy is distraught when he learns that Fanny, formerly a servant of Bathsheba's and the girl he once intended to marry, has died, together with their child. Bathsheba discovers this and after a traumatic scene and Fanny's funeral, Troy leaves Weatherbury and is thought to have drowned.

Boldwood extracts a promise from Bathsheba that she will marry him if Troy does not return after seven years. He holds a party at which he intends to announce their engagement. Troy arrives disguised at the party and claims Bathsheba. Boldwood, driven to the brink of insanity by Troy's reappearance, shoots him and gives himself up to justice.

The novel ends with Bathsheba seeking out Gabriel, who has expressed his intention of emigrating, having given up hope of ever capturing her. The two marry. Bathsheba is a more mature and wiser woman by the end of the novel, very different from the vain young girl who had rejected Gabriel four years earlier.

■ Who's who in
Far From the Madding Crowd

This is a brief overview of each of the major characters. You should use it as a starting point for your own studies of characterisation. For each aspect of a character mentioned, you should look in your text for evidence to support or contradict the views expressed here, and, indeed, your own views as well.

Gabriel Oak

Gabriel is expert as shepherd and farmer: his name symbolises strength and endurance. His love for Bathsheba is honest, unromantic and, above all, steadfast and patient. He is unselfish, and resourceful. He is able to withstand misfortune in all areas of his life. Gabriel is the counterweight to all the other major characters. Hardy has created an idealised character, a man in harmony with Nature, who embodies the countryside's legacy of tradition, simple values and honest living.

However, Hardy does not always take Gabriel Oak too seriously. In particular, in the beginning, his simplicity and social clumsiness are a cause of humour, in incidents such as the gift of the lamb and the proposal. At first he seems in some ways younger than his 28 years. Do you think he changes in the course of the novel? Does he just grow in stature with maturity and authority?

Bathsheba Everdene

Bathsheba is a complex character and her gradual development is central to the progress of the novel. The early chapters stress her high-spirited and independent nature, as well as her vanity and capriciousness. The replies she makes to Gabriel and her attitude towards him are sometimes blameworthy, as is her irresponsibility in her initial dealings with Boldwood. In the central chapters she shows herself to be capable, brave and self-reliant, struggling against multiplying disasters which have their origins in her earlier immaturity. Emotional immaturity leads her into two disastrous relationships – with Boldwood and with Troy. As her marriage to Troy turns bitter, she holds the reader's sympathy through her resourcefulness. Hardy makes it clear that Bathsheba's character includes both fine feelings and faults. By the end of the novel she has revealed an inner strength by being able to endure Troy and Fanny being buried together, and she recognises her need for and love of Gabriel, who has remained loyal and steadfast.

Mr Boldwood

Boldwood is a well-respected, local gentleman farmer. He has dignity, and is depicted as a good neighbour: he is kind to Fanny and to Gabriel. He is noticeably chivalrous in his attempt to save Bathsheba from finding out the truth about her husband's past. The intensity of his emotions comes as a surprise to the reader; he is obsessed by Bathsheba's capricious valentine, losing his self-control and pursuing her with a single-minded passion to make her his wife. This single-mindedness is a characteristic of his throughout. He devotes himself to work to the extent that he alone fails to notice Bathsheba at the market and later has to seek advice on whether she is beautiful. Having been made aware of her, his love becomes so all-encompassing that he totally neglects his farm. His earnest belief in her silly joke is in keeping with his previous earnest rejection of all frivolity. Compare Boldwood's air of maturity and dignity with the helplessness of his inner life, as shown in all the rich gifts labelled 'Bathsheba Boldwood'.

Sergeant Troy

Troy is a fascinating blend of the attractive and the repulsive. Chapter 25 contains a detailed description of him. His appearance is devastatingly attractive to women and his dashing manner, fluent flattery and skill in swordsmanship enable him to 'assault' and win his chosen prey. He seems to have some strength of character but this is quickly shown to be limited – for example, his initial frankness with

Bathsheba is soon offset by lies; his love for Fanny is undermined by neglect of her, and he cruelly abuses Bathsheba once she is his wife. He enjoys role-playing, but as master of Bathsheba's farm he is irresponsible and indifferent to its success. A close analysis of his character and actions reveals him to be an unprincipled cheat and liar and he neither changes nor develops during the novel.

Fanny Robin

Fanny is a young country girl and one of Bathsheba's servants. She is in love with Troy and naively expects him to arrange a date for their wedding. He seems to be willing, but is vague about the details. When the appointed time arrives, Fanny goes to the wrong church. This angers Troy and he rejects her. Pregnant and alone, Fanny loses her job and her exhausted trudge to the workhouse is unforgettably poignant. Her story affects the other characters through her link with Troy and her death is a pivotal moment in the story. Her character is drawn simply, showing her naive honesty and her forlorn faith in her lover. Fanny's significance in the novel is considerable, although her actual appearances are few. For instance, there are no scenes which fully reveal Troy's love for her until she is dead and all that love can do is to help blight Bathsheba's marriage. She is also a major part of Hardy's social comment: as the 'fallen' working-class female tragically punished by Victorian morality. You might like to consider how her name hints at her character: you will find that most of the characters have names that suggest their status or personality, though few are as clear-cut as 'Oak'.

■ Themes in
Far From the Madding Crowd

Love and marriage

Love and marriage

Hardy's novel shows us both the positive and negative aspects of love. Gabriel Oak's love for Bathsheba is honest, steadfast and, above all, founded upon real understanding. Bathsheba rejects Gabriel because she does not love him, and her behaviour in the first part of the novel reveals her ignorance of men and the ways of love. In Fanny we see a victim of love; innocent in a different way from Bathsheba, she is totally unable to cope with a man like Troy. Boldwood symbolises the destructive nature of obsessive love, a love which destroys him and comes close to doing the same to Bathsheba. In Troy we see the face of arrogant sexuality which is attractive in its spontaneity but destructive in its fickleness and its lack of endurance. By the end of the novel, Bathsheba has learned through painful experience to value Gabriel's unswerving love in the face of all adversity. They are 'such tried good friends'.

The theme of marriage provides a framework for Bathsheba's development: her suitors' behaviour tests her poise, her independence, her courage and her final maturity. The destructive power of sex is highlighted by Bathsheba's innocence in the early part of the novel, and by the difficulty she has in coping with her relationships with Troy and with Boldwood in the later chapters. Boldwood's obsessive love is a major example of the havoc caused by sexual desire, whilst Fanny's pregnancy is another warning of the danger of passion.

Nature and rural life

Nature and rural life

Every major scene and incident in the story has the force of Nature as its background, and often it plays an integral part in the action. Nature is depicted as an unrelenting and uncontrollable force. Its harsh side is shown in incidents like the loss of Gabriel's flock and the storm which might have destroyed Bathsheba's ricks. When characters face despair and disillusion, it is often near damp, dark and sinister places which reflect their emotions. The calm face of nature, with its warm spring, summer, harvest-time, and bright starlit winters is important in creating the mood and atmosphere which both support and interpret the action of the story. Of the main characters, only two are really in tune with their natural environment: Gabriel and Bathsheba. Note Gabriel's mental attitude to the traumas and disasters which afflict him. He is steadfast and dependable, like the oak tree from which he gets his name. The weather is shown in three ways in the novel: as part of the natural setting, giving tone and life to the changing seasons; as part of the uncontrollable force of Nature or Fate, as seen in the storm which threatens Bathsheba's ricks and her livelihood; lastly as symbolic of the plight, hopes or fate of the characters, as, for example, the rain on Fanny's grave or the sun in Bathsheba's eyes.

The story begins in December and ends just after December some four years later. During this period, it is not so much the passing of hours and minutes that is important as the slow movement of season passing into season, forming a background to the play of the characters' passions.

Gabriel first proposes to Bathsheba in the winter, and is rejected. With the coming of spring we see the beginnings of Boldwood's obsession, originating from Bathsheba's thoughtless valentine and stimulated by her vanity. Summer sees the heightening of his passion, but it is Troy who wins 'the harvest', with his marriage to Bathsheba in mid-July. As autumn turns to winter, Fanny's life comes to an end. As the year draws to its close, we see the destruction of both Troy and Boldwood. With the new year, Bathsheba faces a new life, with new values and new expectations. For her and Gabriel it represents a new beginning and a time for new growth.

There are three major 'sheep' scenes: the destruction of Gabriel's flock, the saving of Bathsheba's flock by Gabriel, and the sheep-shearing where Gabriel and Bathsheba are joined for a moment in one of the great pastoral set-pieces depicting the idyllic aspect of the countryside. These scenes drive forward the action of the novel, point up the characters' emotions, thoughts and desires, and reflect the sympathetic presence of the seasons in which they occur. Gabriel's loss of one flock and saving of another illustrate both the countryman's stoical acceptance of misfortune and his skill in adapting to his environment.

Depth and strength is added to the novel through the characterisation of the rustics. They represent the time-honoured rituals, customs and work practices of an agricultural community. Hardy's novel is concerned not so much with the real hardships commonly experienced by Victorian agricultural workers as with their symbolic presence in a world soon to change with the growth of technology and industry. He concentrates on their humour, warmth, wit and language which set them in comfortable co-existence with the natural world. The rustics also provide comic relief in a sombre and occasionally melodramatic novel.

The rustics are not central to the action, but are an essential thread running through the novel. They counterpoint, link, and comment upon its major aspects. Rural life is the essence of the novel. Against this backdrop of country life, customs, work, celebrations and natural disasters, the action takes place and the characters develop.

Structure

The serialisation of the story meant that the author had to encourage his readers to purchase the next instalment. This was done in a variety of ways: by an unresolved mystery, by developing a relationship which the readers wished to see further explored, or by the introduction of a catastrophe – natural or man-made. The effects of serialisation are shown by moments of great suspense in the novel.

An important structural theme is that of death. The destruction of Gabriel's flock seems to destroy his hopes of marrying Bathsheba, but ironically it sets him on the road to Weatherbury, where he meets her again. The death of an uncle gives Bathsheba her inheritance, which initially takes her away from Gabriel but actually ensures that they will meet again. Fanny dies because she is a victim of society, and of her own innocence and ignorance, but her death helps to open Bathsheba's eyes to Troy's true nature. Troy dies in the heat of the moment – appropriate to the way he has lived – at the hand of a man possessed by an uncontrollable passion. The deaths of both Boldwood and Troy leave the way open for the fulfilment of Gabriel's hopes.

The colour red is an important linking image. Troy's dazzling red uniform helps the reader see the evil in Troy, not in the black sombre tones of the powers of darkness, but in 'illuminated scarlet'. Evil has a brilliant, attractive side, which Bathsheba responds to and which also attracts the reader. The red spot – the seal on the valentine – which so inflames Boldwood's passions, finds its mirror image in the 'red coat' of Troy, which leads Bathsheba into a passionate but ruinous love affair.

Essays/Examiner's tip icon

This icon is used to draw attention to a section of the **Text commentary** that is particularly relevant to either the section on **How to write a coursework essay** or to the section on **How to write an examination essay**. Each time it is used, a note identifies which section it relates to and adds a comment, quotation or piece of advice.

■ Text commentary

Chapter 1

Gabriel Oak is a young bachelor farmer, a strong, sensible, hardworking man who is at one with his environment. One December morning he sees a handsome young woman seated on a wagon amongst her belongings. He observes certain aspects of her character, revealed in arguing over a twopence toll and then viewing herself with satisfaction in her mirror.

The naming of Farmer Oak

It is no accident that Farmer Oak is named as he is. As you read the novel you will become aware of his durability and strength – characteristics of the oak tree. In the name 'Oak', we also see the coming together of man and nature. It is a feature of the novel that the drama is played out against the background of nature and the cycle of the seasons. Gabriel's Christian name is that of an Archangel. This might suggest the mixture of strength and power with goodness and meekness which will help him to withstand the trials that come his way.

Note how Gabriel's character 'stood in the scale of public opinion'. He is predictable and dependable; people around him may change, but he does not. His durability is also shown in his manner of dress – 'any weaknesses' being compensated for by 'unstinted dimensions and solidity'. Like Nature, he is not easily moved. He will survive the ravages of time, ready to resume life, just as the countryside remains after the violence of storms.

Gabriel's watch, intellect and emotions

Gabriel's 'watch' is only really useful for telling the minutes: his life is ruled by a much slower and majestic 'time-piece' – that of Nature. The story follows the rhythms of life in the countryside, where the rising and setting of the sun, the passage of the seasons, and the uncertainties of the weather are masters of time and man. Gabriel's intellect and emotions 'were clearly separated'. As you read the story, consider the extent to which this natural rhythm protects Gabriel against the tribulations he faces. If he had been perhaps less stolid and more emotional, might he have gained his heart's desire a little earlier? Compare his emotional stability with the lack of it in Mr Boldwood, and with the calculating and volatile nature of Sergeant Troy.

Bathsheba's vanity

We first see Bathsheba secretly admiring herself in a mirror. As the novel

progresses, consider whether this vanity is a major fault in her character. There is a great deal of peering through windows and looking in mirrors in the course of the story. See if you can identify the characters most given to this and ask yourself what it tells you about them.

Bathsheba seems attracted to bright colours. Notice how the sun turns her crimson jacket into a 'scarlet glow'. There is an implied criticism of her character here. The phrase 'Woman's prescriptive infirmity' is a key to the novel's action. Think about how much of the anguish suffered by the three main male characters – and by Bathsheba herself – is caused by this 'infirmity'. Note the prophetic phrases 'dramas in which men would play a part' and 'hearts lost and won' in this context.

Notice the final word of Chapter 1: 'vanity'. Hardy has established some of the features of two of the main characters and made us curious about development of the relationship between the 'solid citizen' Oak, and this vain but handsome girl.

Chapter 2

Gabriel Oak has his own small sheep farm on Norcombe Hill. The landscape's sounds and sensations are strikingly described. Gabriel has a small hut from which he works, tending his flock with skill and care. During the night he notices a light coming from a small shed on the hillside. Inside are two women nursing a cow with a newborn calf. He recognises one of the women as the girl he saw in the wagon. This is the second time he has observed her without her knowledge.

Nature as background

The opening of this chapter is the first detailed description of the countryside. Throughout the novel a balance is carefully maintained between great pastoral descriptions which set the scene and descriptions of characters and incident. Note the language used to describe winter: 'decaying', 'blasts', 'smote', 'weakening moan', 'dead multitude'. Note the reference to the 'desolating wind' which will later contribute to Gabriel's near-suffocation and the loss of his sheep.

Nature and rural life

There is a contrast between the sounds created by the wind and those made by Gabriel's flute. The sounds that come from Gabriel's 'Ark' (his hut) are to be found 'nowhere in the wind'. Gabriel's Ark represents the calmness and integrity of his character. Again, note the Biblical imagery surrounding Gabriel.

Gabriel and nature

Gabriel's 'special power, morally, physically and mentally, was static, owing little or nothing to momentum as a rule'. This is the root of Gabriel's ability to stand apart from the crowd. He is a man who is part of the greater forces linking all living things with nature.

Notice the images here which have Gabriel as their pivot: first we are given a detailed description of the contents of Gabriel's earthly Ark, then the glories of the winter sky and its stars are described: Gabriel, the lamb he has saved, and its mother are placed between the two.

Gabriel and Bathsheba: social class

In Victorian times social class was considered of great importance, even in a community where the very rich were not to be found and where farm-work was a uniting factor. At Weatherbury there will be a social gulf between Gabriel and Bathsheba. Note that this gulf is much less here: people call him 'Farmer' Oak and Bathsheba has work to do just as he has (with cows instead of sheep). Though she is better educated, he is, at this time, more prosperous (see Chapter 4).

Chapter 3

Oak sees the girl out riding the next morning; he observes her skill and her obvious enjoyment of freedom from social restraint. He returns the hat which she has lost but, on the days that follow, she does not speak to him. One night Gabriel falls asleep in his hut, forgetting to leave the ventilating hole open. It is only the girl's chance and timely intervention which saves him from suffocation. In the conversation which follows she teases him and refuses to tell him her name.

Bathsheba teases Gabriel

Bathsheba was embarrassed at Gabriel having seen her ride 'without decorum'. This is another example of her 'vanity'.

Gabriel, revived by Bathsheba, awakes to find his head cradled on her lap. Much later in the novel she cradles Troy's head in her lap, but is not able to revive him. Bathsheba teases Gabriel in the way she lets him hold her hand and she suggests that he might want to kiss it. Her attitude towards Gabriel, a man she has just saved from death, demonstrates a certain thoughtless flirtatiousness. Gabriel's suggestion that she will not retain her maiden name long is perhaps a judgement on his part about her character. You will notice that early on Gabriel does not assume the totally dependable character of later in the novel: do you think his near-suffocation here and the deaths of the sheep in Chapter 5 are just bad luck or is there an element of youthful carelessness?

Chapter 4

Gabriel's interest in the girl develops. He decides he will ask her to be his wife. An orphaned lamb gives him the opportunity to visit her to offer the lamb as a gift. The girl's aunt tells him that she is not at home and that she has many suitors. Gabriel starts for home but Bathsheba runs after him. Her intention is to explain that she has not in fact many suitors. Gabriel misinterprets this as encouragement to propose and to set out his plans for their life together. Bathsheba does not relish the prospect of marriage, and tells Gabriel he should find a rich wife who would help him. Gabriel declares he will love her till he dies even though she has refused him.

Bathsheba's name

We now learn Bathsheba's name. As with Gabriel, there are suggestions in her surname, Everdene, of the timeless qualities of nature and her Christian name is Biblical. Bathsheba was the wife of Uriah, who committed adultery with David and later married him after he had her husband killed.

Love

Love is presented in such a variety of forms and with such tragic consequences that it is amusing to note the first marriage proposal occurs in a low-key semi-comic way so early in the novel: Gabriel's love is not yet taken seriously by Bathsheba (or by Hardy?).

Gabriel proposes

Love and marriage

Notice the abruptness with which Gabriel declares his intention to Bathsheba's aunt of asking Bathsheba to marry him, and the almost crude way in which he asks if she has 'got any other young man hanging about her'. On the other hand, the directness of his questions is disarming. He appears, however, to give up his enterprise very easily, and even to disparage the whole affair: 'that was all I came about. I'll take myself off home-along'. For a man who waited to see Bathsheba as keenly as his dog awaits his dinner, he is remarkably sanguine about the rebuff.

Perhaps the hint to his behaviour with Mrs Hurst and his ready acceptance of rejection is given later in the chapter: what are the 'one-and-a-half Christian characteristics too many' that he has?

When Bathsheba runs after him, Gabriel says, 'When we be married ...' Is he being too presumptuous? Or has Bathsheba led him to believe that she will marry him? Bear in mind her comment: 'I never said I was'. Do you think she is unaware of the signals she gives to men?

Bathsheba's response

One of Bathsheba's main faults to act without considering the consequences of her actions. You can make a comparison to the valentine incident: in both cases she causes a reaction that is much more serious than she anticipates: how do you think she wants Gabriel to react to her running after him to correct her aunt's words? Note her independence: 'I hate to be thought of as men's property'.

Gabriel lists the things Bathsheba will have as his wife: a gig, a piano, a 'frame for cucumbers'. Ironically, she does become a 'lady', but not with Gabriel's help.

Bathsheba's 'moral dilemma'

Bathsheba knows that her 'moral dilemma' is of her own making: 'How I wish I hadn't run after you'. She says that she is too independent and needs someone to 'tame' her, that she is better educated than Gabriel, and too poor for him to be worth marrying. Think about the irony of these statements as the novel unfolds.

Independent woman

Bathsheba later has reasons for independence, inheriting a farm, but the quality is already obvious when she is a 'girl' without money. It is shown in her riding and her saving of Gabriel's life as well as in this chapter.

Chapter 5

Time passes and Bathsheba has moved to Weatherbury, twenty miles away. Gabriel's love for her is constant, but he is thankful that he is unmarried when he loses his entire flock and with it his livelihood. There is a powerful description of the dog driving the sheep over the cliff. Gabriel shoots the dog, sells his stock to pay his debts and is left with what he carries.

Disaster strikes

Consider the quiet certainty of Gabriel's attitude to Bathsheba's departure. It merely leads to Gabriel's 'flame' for her burning more finely.

The sympathy which Gabriel feels for the dead ewes and their unborn lambs is overwhelmed a few moments later by the realisation that he is not insured and is therefore now bankrupt. Next, he feels relief that he has no wife to share in the poverty 'now coming upon me'.

The images of death surrounding the pool into which Gabriel stares reflect the tragedy he has suffered. At a later stage in the novel, Bathsheba will look into a pool similarly charged with sinister reflections.

Chapter 6

Gabriel looks for employment at Casterbridge hiring fair. He earns a little money playing his flute but, still without work, he sets out at night to walk to the next fair near Weatherbury. He overhears two carters talking about the vanity of a lady who owns a farm nearby. Gabriel sees a fire burning in the distance and goes to help. He organises the systematic quenching of the fire in the hay-rick. The young woman farmowner has watched him from a distance and sends words of thanks. Gabriel hopes she will offer him work. He goes to her and as she lifts her veil he recognises her – Bathsheba.

The hiring fair

The hiring fair was an integral part of the county scene, where men competed to sell their services to the farmers. Failure to find work there would perhaps have left a lesser man than Gabriel feeling humiliated and sorry for himself. Note Gabriel's reaction, however. His natural dignity leads other men to address him as 'Sir'. He feels a 'dignified calm' and an 'indifference to fate'. His 'abasement had been an exaltation and the loss gain'. Failing to gain employment as a bailiff, he adopts the dress of a shepherd, only to be rebuffed again. Note the irony of the assumption that Gabriel was 'too good to be trustworthy'.

Gabriel's ability to overcome hard times is illustrated by his flute-playing. He manages to play with 'Arcadian sweetness', as though he has never known a moment's sorrow.

Bathsheba again

The reader is left in little doubt that the woman the two rustics are talking  about is Bathsheba. Her vanity in constantly admiring herself in the mirror (as in Chapter 1) is reported by the two men. Her playing of the piano contributes to the men's estimation of Bathsheba' vanity, despite their enjoyment of the music. A piano was one of the things Gabriel offered Bathsheba when he proposed.

The scene in the wagon is, in many ways, typical of Hardy's method. Chance and coincidence play a large part in all his novels, though, in a relatively unpopulated country area, the fact that this happens to be Bathsheba's wagon is less unlikely than we might think. Equally typical is the role of the rustics. They serve as a chorus (informing us of what has been happening) and provide humour in speech and characters. Note how quickly the character of Joseph Poorgrass is established through conversation.

Another disaster – this time for Bathsheba

A catastrophe drove Gabriel in the general direction of Weatherbury, and another leads him directly to Bathsheba.

Hardy's description of the light and colour of the rick fire is full of vitality. Gabriel takes charge, showing himself to be a man of action, more commanding and sensible than anyone else at the scene. Gabriel saves Bathsheba's ricks from fire and gains employment as a result. In Chapter 37 he saves her ricks from another element, water.

Examiner's tip
You will need to use quotations to show how the atmosphere is created. Note also the role of the rustics (**Rural life**) as Chorus (telling of Bathsheba in the wagon) and vividly creating atmosphere: 'whizzing his great long arms about like a windmill'.

Chapter 7

Bathsheba agrees to employ Gabriel as shepherd, but delegates the details of hiring to her bailiff, Pennyways. Gabriel is on his way to Warren's Malthouse, where he plans to lodge temporarily, when he meets a frail young woman on the road. She asks him not to tell anyone he has seen her. Gabriel is moved by her agitation and gives her a shilling. As he does so, he notices her racing pulse.

Changed fortunes

Bathsheba experiences mixed emotions at Gabriel's reappearance and changed fortunes. For his part, Gabriel is astonished to see how the 'unpractised girl' has developed into a 'cool and supervising woman'. His conclusion that some women only need an emergency to make them fit to deal with one seems to be true in Bathsheba's case.

Fanny – images of tragedy

Gabriel's meeting with Fanny, late in the evening, and so soon after his encounter with Bathsheba, introduces a note of mystery. Her voice has a 'low dulcet note suggestive of romance'. The chance meeting with this young woman, the hint of romance in her voice, her 'throb of tragic intensity', and the image of a lamb 'overdriven' combine to create an air of suspense and impending tragedy. Gabriel's instincts and Hardy's imagery, 'the penumbra of a very deep tragedy', foreshadow events to come.

Chapter 8

Gabriel is made welcome at the Malthouse. He learns that Bathsheba's parents are dead and that she has inherited the farm from an uncle. There is lively and down-to-earth dialogue between the local characters. They talk of Bathsheba's dismissal of her bailiff, and the disappearance of Fanny Robin, one of Bathsheba's servants. They also speak of a soldier who was Fanny's young man. Bathsheba sends someone to Casterbridge to find out about Fanny. Gabriel goes to lodge at one of the farm workers' homes.

Rustic Life

The chapter begins with the first of a number of long and detailed 'rustic conversations'. Close study of them reveals how well these people are in tune with the natural world by which they earn their livelihood. Hardy demonstrates familiarity with their lives, but be aware that this is a somewhat idealised picture of rural life. It does not describe the difficulties and suffering of the peasant classes at this time.

Nature and rural life

The smallness of the rustics' world is shown by the maltster's ability to recall Gabriel's forebears without hesitation. The long lives they apparently lead ('a young man about sixty-five', 'Billy, a child of forty'), put us in mind of the Bible's long-lived patriarchs.

Hardy describes each rustic character in detail, noting their particular traits. Close attention to the details builds an intimate picture of the rustic community. Many of the characters are distinguished by one striking characteristic, so that, though not profound, characterisation is instant and vivid. How would you define the characters of Joseph Poorgrass, Henery Fray and Laban Tall, for instance? Much is made of anecdote: how do you react to Jan Coggan's story of Joseph Poorgrass and the owl – and to Joseph's response to it?

Belonging

As with Gabriel's forebears, the rustics' long memories enable them to recall the Everdene family history, placing Bathsheba in the same rural background as Gabriel.

The description of the years the maltster has lived in the small area, which has been his whole world, emphasises the closeness of this community. Bathsheba and Gabriel are part of it, but Boldwood and Troy are strangers.

Rural life

The scene at the maltster's is a typical Hardy invention. Simple verbal comedy, sharply defined comic characters and traditional stories provide entertainment, but the rustics also function as a chorus, passing on news and enabling Gabriel's character to emerge.

Foreshadowing the future

The interlude with the rustics is brought to an end with two major events, both calculated to set the rustics' tongues wagging. The mysterious girl we met at the end of Chapter 8 is identified, although the reason for her disappearance is yet to be disclosed, and Bathsheba's bailiff is caught stealing. The first reference to a soldier is made, and there is prophetic irony in Bathsheba's hope that Fanny will come to no harm through him.

Gabriel's library

Gabriel is not well educated, but he is far from ignorant. His small collection of books is challenging and valuable. What impression is given by the mixture of the practical, the religious and the imaginative in his library?

Chapter 9

Bathsheba sorts through her late uncle's papers and belongings with the help of her personal maid, Liddy. A man on horseback calls; he is a neighbour and a rich farmer in his middle years, called Mr Boldwood. He has come to pay his respects and to inquire after Fanny. Bathsheba refuses to see him, as she feels she is not dressed to receive callers. The women talk of love, admirers and marriage. Liddy asks Bathsheba if she has ever had a proposal. Bathsheba admits that she has, but does not name her admirer. The farmhands arrive to collect their wages.

Bathsheba's 'romantic possibilities'

When she hears there is a gentleman caller, Bathsheba is described as 'fluttering under the onset of a crowd of romantic possibilities', but there is no evidence that she is expecting anyone at this time, nor that she has formed any romantic attachments in the short period she has been at Weatherbury. Her excitement is caused by her own emotional and romantically inclined nature.

Bathsheba's decision not to receive Mr Boldwood again shows she is vain about her appearance. The discussion between Bathsheba and Liddy begins by describing Mr Boldwood's interest in Fanny's welfare but soon turns to the topic of his eligibility. Again, note the flirtatious side of Bathsheba's nature.

Liddy's response when Bathsheba confides that she refused to marry a man because of his lack of social standing, is not exactly complimentary: 'Kiss my foot, sir; my face is for mouths of consequence'. Is this a fair description of Bathsheba's reaction to Gabriel's proposal?

Chapter 10

Bathsheba informs her workers of Bailiff Pennyways' dismissal, and of her intention to run the farm herself. She talks to each worker and pays the wages which are due, plus some bonuses. Gabriel is treated formally and given Cain Ball as his under-shepherd. News is brought that Fanny Robin has left Casterbridge with a sergeant of the dragoons. Bathsheba sends this information on to Boldwood. She informs the group of workers of her intention to work hard and make her farm a success. She leaves the room with a royal grace which Liddy copies.

Taking charge

By taking over the running of the farm, Bathsheba demonstrates unusual independence for a woman of her time. Note how the men are amazed at her forwardness. The men's reactions to her make for much humour in this chapter, notably Henery Fray's attempts to insert himself into the vacant role of bailiff and Susan Tall's refusal to allow her husband a mind of his own. Bathsheba's generosity to the workers contrasts with Chapter 1 when she argued over a twopence toll. Has she changed, or is it just that her circumstances have changed? Perhaps a new aspect of her character is emerging.

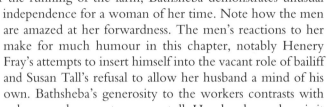

When Bathsheba asks Gabriel if he 'well understands' his duties, is she being deliberately insulting or does she know of his lost flock and wonder at his competence? Perhaps the comment that she has risen in social status and now demonstrates a 'proportionate increase of arrogance and reserve' is the key. Perhaps Bathsheba feels the need to establish her authority straight away and overdoes it a little. Certainly she is asserting her independence and making it clear that any previous relationship between them entitles Gabriel to no special position in her household.

Chapter 11

Fanny approaches Melchester Barracks on a snowy night. There she communicates with Troy through a window. He appears unwilling to arrange their wedding and tries to delay it. Finally, he agrees to call on her at her lodgings the next day .

Troy and Fanny

Note that again a matter of a sombre nature is presaged by 'darkness'. Fanny is usually pictured alone – an outsider and homeless. Darkness and stormy weather often surround her. The grimness of the scene outside the barracks contrasts with the cheerful mockery within (Troy's fellow-soldiers find the prospect of him marrying highly amusing); her earnestness contrasts with his excuses. Names in this novel are usually significant: what is the effect of 'Frank' as Troy's first name?

Chapter 12

Bathsheba demonstrates her ability to carry out her farm's business as she negotiates prices at the Casterbridge Corn Exchange. All admire her, with one notable exception: the unmarried Farmer Boldwood seems indifferent to women.

Bathsheba 'performs' at the Corn Exchange

We have already seen how Bathsheba established her position at her own farm. Here, at the Corn Exchange amongst experienced farmers, her task is even harder. Note how she prepares herself: being 'prettily and even daintily dressed' no doubt helps her own morale, but she will require much more than that to establish her credibility with these men.

The sensuousness of Bathsheba's appearance and manner as she moves through the crowd of farmers, shows the devastating effect she can have on men and helps to explain her effect on Boldwood later. Notice the efficient way in which Bathsheba manages her dealings in the Corn Exchange. It is another indication of shrewd business-sense. However, there is prophetic irony in one farmer's assessment of Bathsheba as 'headstrong' and in his comment: 'she'll soon get picked up'.

Boldwood: 'Pre-eminently' dignified

Remember Bathsheba's first impression of Boldwood: 'erect in attitude', 'quiet in demeanour' and 'pre-eminently' dignified when, later, he is reduced to a deranged man, and driven to shoot Troy. Consider whether his later loss of control is justified by what he has suffered, and evaluate Bathsheba's involvement in it.

Note how Boldwood ignores Bathsheba. His aloofness intrigues her, and she interprets it as romantic. He offends her vanity and she wants him to notice her.

Chapter 13

Bathsheba and Liddy decide to play an old, superstitious game which uses a Bible and key to divine the future. Marks on the pages suggest the Bible has been used for this purpose many times. Liddy, aware that Boldwood is on Bathsheba's mind, suggests that instead of directing the valentine she is writing to a small child, she should send it to Boldwood. This is undertaken in a spirit of jest.

A valentine

Liddy remarks that Boldwood did not look at Bathsheba once during the church service that morning. Liddy's attempts to make Bathsheba confess an interest in Boldwood are as idle and as unthinking as her mistress's behaviour throughout the chapter. Yawns and indecision, choices made by chance (even the fatal 'MARRY ME' seal), show how far from earnest is their mood.

Love and marriage

Liddy's comment that Boldwood will 'worry to death…' when he receives the valentine from Bathsheba is full of irony,

22

given the eventual, tragic outcome. From this point in the novel, Bathsheba suffers the consequences of her capricious act.

Love
The variety of love takes on potentially dangerous strands. In between chapters revealing Troy's cruel neglect of Fanny, Bathsheba's irresponsibility and Boldwood's obsessive response a tragic process starts. Notice that Gabriel for now is reduced to observer/adviser.

Chapter 14

Boldwood is deeply affected by the valentine and ponders on the mystery of who sent it. He is unable to sleep and takes a walk at dawn. He meets a postman who gives him, by mistake, a letter for Gabriel. After opening it, Boldwood realises the error and sets off to deliver it to its rightful owner.

Boldwood's reaction to the valentine

Again, evening is the setting for an event which will prove tragic. Notice the prophetic irony of the red seal becoming like 'a blot of blood' in Boldwood's eye. The arrival of the valentine has a dramatic effect which is perhaps surprising on Boldwood given his supposed indifference to eligible young women. It helps to prepare us for the dramatic events which follow.

The imagery – a sunrise that resembles sunset over Weatherbury Upper Farm – mirrors the confusion caused by the valentine. It was sent in jest, but was received in earnest.

Chapter 15

Some farm workers in the local tavern talk about Bathsheba's inability to run the estate – because she is a woman. They concede that she is educated and clever, but criticise her vanity and extravagance. Gabriel warns them that they will have to reckon with him if they criticise her again in his presence. Boldwood arrives and gives Gabriel his letter. It is from Fanny Robin. She returns his money and tells him she will soon be married to Sergeant Troy, whom she believes to be a man of honour. When Gabriel shows Boldwood the letter, Boldwood doubts Troy's integrity. Boldwood shows Gabriel the valentine. Gabriel is able to identify the handwriting: it is Bathsheba's.

A judgement on Bathsheba

Here is another conversation between the rustics, again providing an insight into their lives. Henery Fray comments that Bathsheba's problems stem from a mixture of her pride and vanity and from her headstrong nature. His judgement accords in part with what we have seen of her so far, but it is not to be trusted. Henery's comments about Bathsheba are based solely on her treatment of him: why is he convinced that she cannot run the farm herself? The humour comes from his vanity and the sympathy of his cronies.

Gabriel's loyalty to Bathsheba

The simple and open honesty of Gabriel's love for Bathsheba comes across when he defends her honour and reputation, threatening the rustics if they should dare to speak ill of her. Gabriel defends her even though he seems to have accepted that his hopes of marrying her are gone.

Tangled webs

Different threads of the plot are gathered here. The misdirected letter has brought Gabriel and Boldwood together and causes Bathsheba's valentine and Fanny and Troy's relationship to be openly discussed.

Fanny's letter shows her simplicity and her trust in both Gabriel and Troy, a trust which is betrayed by Gabriel immediately, when he shows the letter to Boldwood, and by Troy later.

Boldwood's concern for Fanny's welfare is based on his knowledge of Troy. Ironically, Boldwood's good sense in commenting on Fanny deserts him in his own case: he can see that Fanny is 'a silly girl', but cannot comprehend the possibility of Bathsheba's trivial behaviour.

The realisation that Boldwood's valentine came from Bathsheba comes as a blow for Gabriel. However, it is Boldwood who finds the news 'torture'.

■ Self-test questions Chapters 1–15

Uncover the plot

Delete two of the alternatives given, to find the correct plot. Beware possible misconceptions and muddles.

Gabriel Oak observes a beautiful girl and particularly notices her modesty/vanity/pride. Later, she refuses his proposal of marriage indignantly/sadly/with a laugh. All Gabriel's sheep are killed because of his dog/disease/a storm and he is forced to seek employment, finding a place as bailiff/shepherd/farmworker with Bathsheba, his love, now a prosperous farmer. Her friend/youngest servant/companion, Fanny Robin, has run away to join her soldier/farmer/lawyer sweetheart. Bathsheba dismisses her bailiff for thieving/bad management/drunkenness and deals directly with the other farmers; only Boldwood/Oak/Troy ignores her. She discusses him with Maryann/Temperance/Liddy and after long thought/idly/as a revenge sends him a valentine. The farmer's attention is drawn and he asks Liddy/Gabriel/Fanny to identify Bathsheba's writing.

Who? What? Why? When? Where? How?
1 Who was so fond of his wife that 'he used to light the candle three times at night to look at her'?
2 Whom does Gabriel help during his first hours as Bathsheba's employee?
3 What does Bathsheba do at the beginning of the novel when she thinks that she is unobserved, and what does Gabriel conclude?
4 What event leads to Bathsheba becoming mistress of the farm?
5 Why does she refuse Gabriel's proposal?
6 Why does she particularly notice Boldwood in the cornmarket?
7 Where does Gabriel first speak to Bathsheba?
8 Where do Bathsheba's workers go to drink?
9 How does Gabriel come to lose his farm?
10 How does Bathsheba make the decision to send Boldwood the valentine?

Who is this?
1 '…when his friends and critics were in tantrums, he was considered rather a bad man; when they were pleased, he was rather a good man; when they were neither, he was a man whose moral colour was a kind of pepper-and-salt mixture.'
2 'He was erect in attitude and quiet in demeanour. One character pre-eminently marked him – dignity'.
3 '(He) exhibited an ebony-tipped nose, surrounded by a narrow margin of pink flesh, and a coat marked in random splotches approximating in colour to white and slaty grey;…'
4 '(She), like a little brook, though shallow, was always rippling;…'
5 'Among these heavy yeomen a feminine figure glided… She moved between them as a chaise between carts, was heard after them as romance after sermons, was felt among them like a breeze among furnaces.'
6 'The voice was unexpectedly attractive; it was the low and dulcet note suggestive of romance; common in descriptions, rare in experience.'
7 ' "Forty, I should say – very handsome – rather stern-looking – and rich" '.

Familiar themes
Nature and the natural world are very important themes in the novel. In the nineteenth century, natural description was often used to indicate human emotion, drama or tragedy. What events do the following descriptions mirror or comment upon and what effect do they have?
1 'If anything could be darker than the sky, it was the wall, and if anything could be gloomier than the wall it was the river beneath.' (Chapter 9)
2 'By the outer margin of the pit was an oval pond, and over it hung the attenuated skeleton of a chrome-yellow moon, which had only a few days to last – the morning star dogging her on the left hand. The pool glittered like a dead man's eye…' (Chapter 5)
3 'Individual straws in the foreground were consumed in a creeping movement of ruddy heat, as if they were knots of red worms, and above shone imaginary fiery faces, tongues hanging from lips, glaring eyes, and other impish forms,… (Chapter 6)
4 '… in general there was here, too, that before-mentioned preternatural inversion of light and shade which attends the prospect when the garish brightness commonly in the sky is found on the earth, and the shades of earth are in the sky. Over the west hung the wasting moon, now dull and greenish-yellow, like tarnished brass.' (Chapter 4)

5   'It was a fine morning, and the sun lighted up to a scarlet glow the crimson
    jacket she wore, and painted a soft lustre upon her bright face and dark hair.
    The myrtles, geraniums, and cactuses packed around her were fresh and
    green, and at such a leafless season they invested the whole concern of
    horses, wagons, furniture, and girl with a peculiar vernal charm.' (Chapter 1)

Prove it!
Bathsheba, unusually independent for a young girl of her time, is much discussed
by other people in the novel. Find a quotation from each of the following chapters
to prove this statement.
1   Chapter 4
2   Chapter 6
3   Chapter 8
4   Chapter 12
5   Chapter 15

Chapter 16

*Troy waits in All Saints' Church for Fanny to arrive for their wedding ceremony. Over
half an hour passes as Troy grows more embarrassed and humiliated. As he leaves,
Fanny arrives, having waited at the wrong church. Troy angrily refuses to arrange a
definite time and place for another ceremony.*

Wedding bells for Fanny and Troy?

Notice how this wedding scene is effectively written against the background
of the leering clock, an image which builds up the tension, with the 'leer'
suggesting that things will not go well.

Troy's words 'And when…' in response to Fanny's question about when
they will marry, are spoken with bitterness and are more
prophetic than he could realise. It becomes obvious from later
events that he does love Fanny. Why then does he treat her
in this way? Is his pride and vanity so cruelly taxed that he is
incapable of doing the right thing now? Troy was obviously
reluctant to marry in Chapter 11, but his intention here (easily

Troy

overcome, as it turns out) is to go through with the ceremony. Why? And
what makes him refuse a second attempt at the marriage service?

Chapter 17

*Boldwood is now obsessed by thoughts of Bathsheba. At the cornmarket on Saturday
morning he gazes rapturously at her and enquires of others if she is considered a great
beauty. Bathsheba feels pleased to have attracted him, but regrets that it was the foolish
valentine which brought this about. They do not speak.*

Paradise lost?

The allusion to Adam's first sight of Eve stresses the growth of Boldwood's
obsession and warns of impending disaster – Adam's Garden of Eden was

destroyed after he had fallen prey to Eve's temptations, and Boldwood's previously well-ordered life will likewise be destroyed.

There is a tremendous contrast between the way Boldwood 'dimly understood' women, and the way he looks at Bathsheba. It is plain that Boldwood has been deeply affected by Bathsheba's thoughtless act.

Bathsheba's problem

'Boldwood's blindness' and 'Bathsheba's insensibility' to the results of 'little beginnings' is the genesis of much of the tragedy that will follow.

Bathsheba recognises, too late, the quandary in which she has placed herself. This creates suspense about how she will resolve her problem.

Chapter 18

Boldwood is a man of some importance in the parish. His land adjoins Bathsheba's. He sees her working in a field and feels compelled to approach and speak to her. Shyness prevents him speaking, but his presence causes Bathsheba embarrassment. Gabriel senses her change of mood. Bathsheba determines to give Boldwood no further reason to think she is interested in him.

Boldwood's torment

As with other characters, the author here gives an insight into Boldwood's

mind. Note the words which surround this description of him: 'cloister', 'celibate', 'meditate', 'passion', 'stillness', 'stern', 'serious'. This is not the man to ignore a valentine. In his description of Boldwood, Hardy presents a man whose emotional balance is precarious. Boldwood's emotional state is mirrored by the natural world: spring is coming and human

passions planted during the winter now start to grow. Boldwood is tellingly described as 'now living outside his defences'. Being in love is a new experience for him.

Bathsheba's resolve

Here is an insight into Bathsheba's concern at the 'flame' she has kindled in Boldwood. She is not a flirt or a schemer, and resolves to do nothing to encourage him further. Ironically this resolution comes too late, and her earlier fears that Boldwood will misinterpret whatever she says are confirmed in tragic circumstances later.

Chapter 19

Boldwood decides he must speak to Bathsheba and seeks her out while she is watching the sheep-washing. He declares his passion and proposes to her. Bathsheba tries to refuse him but out of sympathy for him says she will think about it, leaving him with some hope that she might accept him.

Another proposal for Bathsheba

The rhythms of nature prevent Boldwood from speaking to Bathsheba at first. Boldwood, himself a farmer, has forgotten for the moment the pressures that nature imposes on the farming community. This shows how far his own equilibrium has been disturbed.

The decision that Bathsheba has found so difficult to make is now forced upon her. Perhaps she should have approached Boldwood first and put his mind at rest, before he had time to dwell on the valentine and its implications. She now has to face the consequences of her frivolous act.

Love and marriage

Bathsheba's honest rejection of Boldwood's proposal is tempered with remorse and pity. She is genuinely ashamed of what she has done and the pain she has caused him. Her pity for the man leads her into the fatal mistake of leaving him just a little hope. For a man like Boldwood, this is enough encouragement for him to begin to build his hopes.

Love/Rural life

It is one of Hardy's strengths that his focus is, in some ways, fairly narrow. Key moments in the rejection or acceptance of love are set against the work of the farm year. At other times love can lead to dedication (Oak) or neglect (Boldwood) in work.

Chapter 20

Though not in love with Boldwood, Bathsheba knows that a marriage to him would be financially and socially advantageous. Even so, she is doubtful whether it would be a wise move. She enjoys her independent control of the farm and does not feel the need to marry. She asks Gabriel for his opinion while they are grinding shears together. Gabriel's candid reply makes Bathsheba angry and she dismisses him.

Bathsheba's novel position

Mr Boldwood

The start of this chapter explores some motives behind the wish to marry. It highlights the unusual position in which Bathsheba finds herself. She is an independent woman, with authority in a man's world. Her position 'was a novel one' and she is torn between wanting to keep her independence and feeling she ought to marry Boldwood because she 'began the game'.

Honest, but unsympathetic answers

We frequently see Gabriel and Bathsheba together at work, but this is the first instance of physical contact between them. Gabriel takes the opportunity to hold her hands for longer than is necessary and she asserts her right to free them. Bathsheba tries to gauge from Gabriel the general reaction to her meeting with Boldwood. Perhaps she is concerned about the potential scandal and damage to her reputation; perhaps, subconsciously, she is interested in Gabriel's reaction.

Unhappy with Gabriel's response, Bathsheba's insistence on being properly addressed as 'Miss Everdene' is a fairly unsuccessful attempt to maintain her dignity.

Despite her annoyance, Bathsheba perseveres and demands Gabriel's opinion of her conduct. Gabriel either seems to be bereft of tact, or perhaps he feels that, unlike Bathsheba's response to Boldwood, an honest question requires an honest answer. But having given the answer, he then rubs salt in her wounds by saying that his honest answer 'would do good'.

In this emotionally fraught situation, Gabriel's maturity is evident. His extra eight years over Bathsheba is much more apparent than in the opening chapters or in the scenes of farm business. She can only see his motivation as being resentment of her not marrying him; he conveys a genuine agitation at the way she is harming Boldwood. Despite her pride she cannot conceal her emotions; despite his true feelings he manages to stay calm when agreeing he does not wish to marry her. How does his calm affect Bathsheba?

Bathsheba's reaction to Gabriel's frankness shows her at her most vulnerable. She has yet to attain the maturity to deal with the situation without losing her temper, and she dismisses him because he has affronted her dignity. Note how Gabriel accepts the blow with 'placid dignity'.

Chapter 21

The next day, Bathsheba's sheep fall ill. They have wandered into a field of clover which, when eaten by sheep, distends their stomachs, ultimately causing death. This needs very skilled and speedy treatment. Gabriel is the only man in the locality able to cure them, but he refuses to help unless he is asked politely. Bathsheba has to plead with him. He cures most of the flock. Bathsheba asks him to stay on as shepherd and he agrees.

A quandary for Bathsheba

The narrative is tied closely the rhythms of nature and to the life and work of the farmer. When Gabriel and Bathsheba re-establish contact, their relationship has undergone a quite radical change as a result of what Gabriel said about Bathsheba's conduct.

Remember that it was the destruction of his flock, shortly after Bathsheba had rejected his proposal of marriage, that made Gabriel glad he had no wife and drove him from his farm to Weatherbury and to Bathsheba. Now it is the threat to her flock, shortly after she has 'rejected' his services, that brings them together again. Their lives are tied to the land and, through it, to each other.

Nature and rural life Note that Farmer Boldwood begins to neglect his farm as his obsessive love for Bathsheba grows, and Troy too neglects Bathsheba's farm, once he has married her. There is no such neglect on either Gabriel's or Bathsheba's part.

The farm labourers' respect for Gabriel's skills as a shepherd is another quandary for Bathsheba. Should she swallow her pride and send for Gabriel? In fact, the way she asks for his help is an attempt both to satisfy her vanity and to save her sheep. But Gabriel's reply is not calculated to please Bathsheba, though it is perhaps a suitable response to her rude and thoughtless message. Gabriel's reply, 'as becomes any 'ooman begging a favour', shows the same apparent lack of respect as his opinion of her conduct with Boldwood. He is not prepared to allow the rustics to indulge in any scurrilous gossip about Bathsheba, but when he thinks she is in the wrong he does not hesitate to tell her so.

'Shall I beg to a man who has begged to me?' is possibly the crux of the matter for Bathsheba's pride. There is something pointed in the way one of the flock, as if in reply, 'sprang into the air, and fell dead'. The incident puts 'airs' and the question of who shall 'beg' into perspective.

Examiner's tip

For the essay title on page 66 you are asked to examine three scenes. In preparing for an examination you should make sure of your knowledge of these key events which are relevant for many essays: this section also has invaluable material for all three **Coursework essays**.

Gabriel to the rescue

This is the second of three occasions when Gabriel rescues Bathsheba from a natural disaster. He saved her ricks from fire in Chapter 6 and saves them from a storm in Chapter 37. Each time, a new stage in their relationship is reached.

Bathsheba knows she can manipulate Gabriel with her femininity, but equally she knows the limitations on what she can make him do. In this respect he is still very much his own man. The scene is set for Gabriel's advancement.

Chapter 22

Early June is sheep-shearing time. Bathsheba watches; Oak's speed and skill impress her but the atmosphere changes with the arrival of Boldwood. Bathsheba goes with Boldwood to view his flock. The farm workers conclude that there will be a marriage soon. Gabriel disputes this.

Promise of things to come

The sheep shearing is a great event in the farming calendar. The image of

Nature and rural life

nature, rich with the promise of good things to harvest and with its 'racing currents of juice', echoes the ripening of the relationships between Bathsheba and the two competitors for her hand, Boldwood and Gabriel.

There is a sense of timelessness in the description of the great barn; similar in form to the neighbouring church and vying with it for antiquity, its use for the age-old practice of sheep-shearing evokes a sense of continuity and of harmony between man and nature. For farmers, sheep-shearing was almost a religious ceremony.

Notice the delicate sensuality of the scene between Bathsheba and Gabriel.

Love and marriage

It is as if the two of them, separated from the other shearers, are in a world of their own. Study the language used to describe the atmosphere of intimacy: 'lopped off… and collar', 'quietly looking on', 'murmured', 'pink flush'. Note Gabriel's reaction, happy to be alone with Bathsheba: his silence 'says much'.

Boldwood's appearance disrupts the happy and sensuous mood of the barn. This change is reflected by a change in language: suddenly we are confronted with the harsh reality of 'rams and old ewes', 'shearlings and hogs'.

Bathsheba displays her vanity, Gabriel defends her

The sudden appearance of Boldwood unsettles Bathsheba and she vents her

Gabriel Oak

displeasure on Gabriel, knowing she is partly responsible for the wound to the sheep he is shearing. Perhaps also her vanity is hurt at being seen so close to Gabriel and working as a common rustic.

Again the rustics comment on the action and again Gabriel defends Bathsheba's reputation against their gossip. Note, however, that Gabriel will soon begin to brood on what he considers to be the injustice done to him. It is interesting to compare Gabriel's introspection with the way Boldwood reacts to the unpredictable Bathsheba.

Chapter 23

The sheep-shearing supper is ready. Bathsheba invites Gabriel to sit at the head of the table. He has to give up this place on Boldwood's arrival. There is traditional music and singing; all make a contribution to this. Later, in the farmhouse, Boldwood again declares his love. Bathsheba promises to consider marrying him and to give her answer by harvest-time. Boldwood is heartened by this.

Bathsheba, Boldwood, Oak and Troy

The shearing supper aligns Bathsheba uneasily with all three of her potential husbands. She has planned that Mr Boldwood will join her and the workers, sitting in state at the bottom of the table. His lateness means that Gabriel has to take the seat ('with great readiness'), only to be literally 'put in his place' when Boldwood arrives. There is tragic irony in Gabriel and Boldwood accompanying Bathsheba as she sings of a gay soldier with a winning tongue seeking a bride.

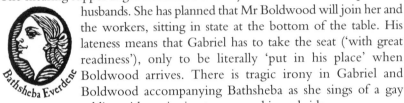

Independent woman

Bathsheba is still in charge of her own destiny, though troubled by how to deal with Boldwood. Note the symbolism of both the men accompanying her song: Boldwood does not sing a duet. But the arrival of Troy will end her control.

Bathsheba has now had two proposals of marriage, both of which she failed to answer immediately. We have seen how Gabriel has coped with rejection. He still loves her, but is content at the moment to defend her reputation, to help her, and to be near her. Boldwood has also been told to wait. But he is no Gabriel Oak. His will never be a patient game of 'wait and see'. Just when it seems Bathsheba might eventually be won by Boldwood, Troy enters the story and sends the action in a different direction.

The rustics: comedy and significance

Hardy enjoys setting highly charged emotional scenes against a background of the tranquillity of rural life. You will doubtless be able to think of many more examples. Here the shearing supper is full of gentle comfortable humour. You are probably familiar enough with the character of Joseph Poorgrass to savour his mixture of triumph and humiliation. His conversation with **Nature and** Jan Coggan about Bailiff Pennyways is a splendidly earnest **rural life** piece of nonsense: praising him immoderately for not stealing anything. However, if you look at the songs sung by Jan and Joseph, you will find that they provide a background commentary to Bathsheba's *The Banks of Allan Water*: all lost love and weeping willows.

Chapter 24

After the sheep-shearing supper, Bathsheba makes her nightly tour of the estate. Passing through the fir plantation she meets a stranger and her dress is caught at the hem in his spur. The man is a soldier – Sergeant Troy. His dashing, teasing manner at once distresses and enchants Bathsheba. She runs home, where Liddy tells her his history and Bathsheba feels she might have been too rude to him.

Bathsheba 'mastered'?

Significantly, Bathsheba has her first encounter with Troy at night. The

Troy

tension is built up by an emphasis on Bathsheba's lack of any fear that what she is doing might be dangerous. As before, when danger or turmoil are present the author's descriptions evoke aspects of the natural world which add to the oppressive atmosphere. The night is as 'black as the ninth plague' and there are 'dead spikelets' and 'mildewed cones'.

Read carefully this encounter between Troy and Bathsheba. Troy makes a distinct appeal to Bathsheba's vanity. What is her response?

Love/Rural life

Note how even this scene, the most obviously romantic encounter, is fitted in to the routine of farm life: Bathsheba's security check. You need to be able to explain how Troy's approach turns her head: count the number of references to 'beauty' or 'beautiful'!

It is revealing how the three men in Bathsheba's life no sooner get into conversation with her than their thoughts seem to turn to marriage. Look back at her conversations with Boldwood and Gabriel to see when they first made direct or oblique references to marriage. Notice the suggestion that she is not averse to being praised nor mastered, two things which neither Gabriel nor Boldwood 'offered'.

Chance and coincidence

Hardy's use of coincidence (sometimes unreasonably condemned as excessive) often turns on misfortunes of timing. Bathsheba has a problem in regard to Boldwood which she may perhaps be able to solve with time: at the crucial point she literally becomes entwined with Troy. Chance also plays a part in the moral degradation of Troy. His treatment of Fanny and Bathsheba is deplorable, but it is not his fault that Fanny mistakes the church or that Bathsheba chooses this time to check the homestead. Do you think that Troy is in any sense a victim of circumstance or is his moral decline inevitable?

Chapter 25

Troy offers his services to Bathsheba to help with the hay-making.

The author's view of Troy

This chapter centres upon a detailed description of Troy. He emerges as a man

who looks neither forward nor back but pursues instant gratification. He lacks finer feelings, lies to women, and relies on flattery and his dashing air of reckless charm. He is not really evil, since his sins stem from his natural impulsiveness and lack of moral discrimination. The description shows Troy

Troy   to be the complete opposite of Gabriel.

Chapter 26

Troy flatters and teases Bathsheba. She in turn teases him and accuses him of leading her on. Suddenly he produces a gold watch and gives it to her, declaring that he loves her. Bathsheba is confused by his advances and refuses the gift, but accepts his offer to help in her fields.

Troy flatters Bathsheba

Bathsheba is confused by Troy's flattering barrage of words. She seems to be faced with some painful choices, torn between establishing her social position, exercising her role as an independent woman, and wanting to hear more.

How sophisticated is Bathsheba Everdene? It is not always easy to tell, partly because she spends so much time among people whose total lack of sophistication makes her appear more worldly. She is very young (20 at the beginning of the novel) and here she is unduly impressed by snatches of French (she only got as far as the verbs), tales of aristocratic connections and so on. There are moments when good sense asserts itself ('Your words are too dashing to be true'), but at the end of the chapter she is hopelessly confused, both about the truth of what he says and about what she has started.

Independent woman/Love

Bathsheba's confusion can be well summarised in many pairs of quotations: e.g. 'I don't allow strangers to be bold and impudent - even in praise of me' (independent, in charge) and 'It doesn't seem quite true to me that I am fascinating' (falling for Troy's flattery).

The gift of the watch is a turning-point in both their lives. Its motto, 'Love yields to circumstances', is an ironic comment on the 'circumstances' of several characters in the novel: Bathsheba, Boldwood, Fanny and Oak.

Chapter 27

Fate takes a hand when Bathsheba is having difficulty with a hive of bees. Troy arrives and is able to do the job for her after she has dressed him in her protective clothing. Troy offers to demonstrate his sword drill to her. Initially she refuses, but is persuaded to meet him in secret.

Summer heat

The season – midsummer – is a fitting backdrop for the development of the

Love and marriage

action. Bathsheba and Troy's love will be as intense and short-lived as the summer heat. It is also fitting that bees, which flit from one flower to another, gathering their honey, are part of the setting for Bathsheba's next encounter with Troy.

'Whimsical fate' dictates that Bathsheba should again be in close physical contact with Troy, as she dresses him in protective clothing. This echoes the scene when Bathsheba and Troy first met.

Chapter 28

In a ferny hollow, the sword drill becomes a direct confrontation between Troy the man and Bathsheba the woman. Troy astonishes and dazzles Bathsheba with his dexterity and magnetism. She falls under the spell of his performance, and his kiss excites her. From now on, Troy is the dominant partner in their relationship.

A masterful demonstration and a capitulation

The association of different times of the day with appropriate dramatic events is continued here with Bathsheba and Troy meeting in the evening.

The author provides a structural link here with the reference to the 'spot of red', a 'spot' which will loom very large in Bathsheba's life. Boldwood saw a spot of red which became larger and more inflamed in his eyes. Do you remember what it was? Is there a parallel here in the way Boldwood reacted to Bathsheba with the way she reacts to Troy?

Troy's sword is 'like a living thing'. His dazzling display of skill symbolises

Troy

Troy's ability to dominate women and leads to the eventual capitulation of Bathsheba. Note those words and phrases which emphasise the sensuousness of this scene and the use of the light image in connection with Troy's masterful swordplay. Bathsheba is, appropriately, dazzled – physically, emotionally and sexually.

Bathsheba, 'overcome by a hundred tumultuous feelings' resulting from the sword drill, is left 'powerless to withstand or deny him'. This is an important moment in their relationship, and you might like to consider whether Bathsheba's behaviour has any parallel with Boldwood's.

With his sword, Troy cuts off a lock of Bathsheba's hair. Later, the fact that he has in his possession a lock of hair which is not Bathsheba's leads to his downfall.

■ Self-test questions Chapters 16–28

Uncover the plot

Delete two of the alternatives given, to find the correct plot. Beware possible misconceptions and muddles.

Boldwood looks properly at Bathsheba and falls in love with her; she is pleased/embarrassed/sorry that she sent the valentine. He asks her to marry him in May/June/July at the sheep-washing/sheepshearing/harvest; she at first refuses with contempt/dignity/mirth but is confused by his vehemence and asks for time to consider. Gabriel/Jack Smallbury/Laban Tall criticises her behaviour and she dismisses him angrily, but is forced to beg him to return when her sheep become ill/escape/need shearing. The shearing takes place in the Great Meadow/the New Barn/the Great Barn and at the shearing supper Boldwood/Gabriel/Troy proposes again and Bathsheba promises him an answer the following day/in a few weeks/in seven years. That same night/a few days later/a few weeks later, while she looks round the farm before going to bed, her dress becomes entangled in Troy's/Coggan's/Pennyways' sword/spur/buttons. He gives her a necklace/his watch/his sword and persuades her to come alone to watch him demonstrate his swordplay/shooting/dancing. He kisses her and she slaps him/runs away/bursts into tears.

Who? What? Why? When? Where? How?

1   Who tells Bathsheba that she has behaved badly to Boldwood?
2   Who helps Bathsheba to hive the bees?
3   What fatal omission does Boldwood make in wooing Bathsheba (according to Hardy)?
4   What causes Gabriel to leave the farm?
5   Why does Gabriel falter during the sheep shearing and wound a sheep?
6   Why does Bathsheba weep when Troy leaves her after his display of swordsmanship?

7　Why is Bathsheba not at home when Boldwood first calls upon her after receiving the valentine?

8　When and where does Boldwood first look properly at Bathsheba?

9　How does Bathsheba react when Boldwood proposes for the second time at the shearing supper?

10　How do Troy and Bathsheba first meet?

Who is this?

1　'…with him the past was yesterday, the future, tomorrow; never, the day after.'

2　' "I know him to be very quick and trim, who might have made his thousands, tike a squire. Such a clever young dand as he is" '

3　'the erratic child of impulse…'

4　'(Her) beauty belonging rather to the demonian than to the angelic school, she never looked so well as when she was angry – and particularly when the effect was heightened by a rather dashing velvet dress, carefully put on before a glass.'

5　'His equilibrium disturbed, he was in extremity at once. If an emotion possessed him at all, it ruled him; a feeling not mastering him was entirely latent.'

Parallel lines

Later in the novel, Hardy writes: '…Troy's deformities lay deep down from a woman's vision, whilst his embellishments were upon the very surface…' (29)

Characters in the novel are not always as they appear to be and there is often a fracture between appearance and reality, or between what people say and what they think. Can you find examples of this relating to the characters below?

1　Bathsheba (18)

2　Gabriel (22)

3　Boldwood (18)

4　Troy (25)

About time

Hardy places his characters and their story against a background of change and continuity; rotating seasons and the seasonal demands of farm work are carefully noted in nearly every chapter and this natural flow is set in the context of ancient time and old certainties. In each of the chapters listed below, find a) the time of year b) the task on the form and c) a piece of natural description.

1　Chapter 18

2　Chapter 19

3　Chapter 22

4　Chapter 27

Open quotes

Complete the following useful quotes; the numbers in brackets refer to the chapters in which they can be found.

1　Bathsheba at first refuses Boldwood's proposal of marriage with the words: 'you are too ……… for me to suit you, sir.' (19)

2　At the shearing supper, Bathsheba sings: 'For his bride ………' (23)

3　Hardy gives a vivid description of the play of Troy's sword round Bathsheba, concluding: 'In short, she was enclosed in ………' (28)

4　When Boldwood falls in love with Bathsheba, there is a change in his appearance. '… his face showed that he was now ………' (18)

5　When Bathsheba becomes literally entangled with Troy, Hardy writes of the soldier: 'His sudden appearance was to darkness what ………' (24)

Chapter 29

Gabriel wants to speak to Bathsheba about her involvement with Troy. They meet one evening and he speaks about her possible marriage to Boldwood. Bathsheba informs him there will be no such marriage and she is angered when Gabriel expresses the view that Troy is unworthy of her. In defence of Troy, Bathsheba says he goes to church regularly although he enters unobserved by a side door. Bathsheba would like to dismiss Gabriel but he reminds her how much she needs his skilled labour. They part, she to meet Troy, he to the church, where he examines the side door. It has not been opened for years. Troy has been lying.

Bathsheba – blinded by love?

There is a detailed description of Bathsheba's motives and character at the start
 of this chapter. Her love for Troy 'was entire as a child's... her culpability lay in her making no attempt to control feeling by... inquiry into consequences'. The latter part of this quotation also applies to her relationship with Boldwood. Remember how she glossed over her own responsibility for the Boldwood situation and its potential consequences, when she spoke to Gabriel in Chapter 20.

If Bathsheba had wanted to, she could easily have discovered the falsity of Troy's claim that he attended church – after all, he is hardly the sort of man to creep humbly into church the back way. But Bathsheba is not really interested in discovering the truth about Troy.

Gabriel declares his undying love for Bathsheba

Gabriel's declaration of his love and his advice as to how Bathsheba should behave brings another command to leave. He shows dignity and a degree of annoyance, and is perhaps a touch more masterful with Bathsheba here than previously. Is he beginning to tire of being so placid and self-effacing? Note the irony that, a moment before, Bathsheba had been praising Troy for his bluntness 'sometimes to the point of rudeness'. Now, she proposes to dismiss Gabriel for the same thing. Her inconsistency reveals her inner struggle.

Chapter 30

Troy is leaving for Bath. Bathsheba goes home and writes to Boldwood, telling him she will not marry him. Overhearing her servants discussing the probability of her marrying Troy, she first tells them she hates him, and then defends him. She confesses to Liddy privately that she is in love with Troy and asks her for reassurance that his bad reputation is undeserved. Liddy promises not to tell anyone of Bathsheba's feelings.

Bathsheba is confused

Bathsheba at last comes to a decision and writes immediately to Boldwood,

Love and marriage

putting an end to their relationship and to his hopes of marriage. Notice the evident confusion in Bathsheba's mind as she manipulates the conversation with her servants, making contradictory statements and talking almost hysterically about her future, even imagining dying in the workhouse. Troy, the man who has driven her to such distraction, will in fact cause Fanny, not Bathsheba to die in the workhouse.

In her desperation, Bathsheba is determined to believe that Troy really is all she wants him to be, even going to the extent of asking Liddy to support her self-deception.

Chapter 31

While out walking next morning, Bathsheba meets Boldwood. He repeats his declaration of love but, although Bathsheba expresses regret for her thoughtlessness and pities him, she refuses to change her mind. When she admits that Troy is the man who has won her affection, Boldwood is enraged, and threatens Troy. All Bathsheba's thoughts are for Troy's safety.

Confrontation between Bathsheba and Boldwood

Evening again, and the scene is set for the storm which is about to break around Bathsheba. Note the ominous imagery of the 'lairs of fierce light' which appear before her in the sky as she leaves the house.

Love and marriage

The flaws in Boldwood's character are shown in the way he demeans himself before Bathsheba, pleading that she should not 'throw (him) off'. Note the balance in the dialogue between Bathsheba and Boldwood. Many of his arguments are well reasoned and justified in their accusations of her unfaithfulness. However, though his statements are often reasonable, his moods reflect anything but reason. Hardy mentions his 'unreasonable anger' and he moves from violent expressions of love to self-revulsion to furious anger, most dangerously directed at Troy. Everything is said in passion and he wavers between 'recklessly renouncing' her and 'labouring humbly' for her. How would you assess Boldwood's state of mind in this chapter?

Love

One of the most difficult and interesting characters to analyse is Boldwood: when he is reasonable, he is very reasonable, but this conceals a dangerously unbalanced personality. Note here the difference between reasonable arguments and crazy fixations.

In contrast, Bathsheba's replies are brief. She is not in control of the situation but she is attempting to be honest with Boldwood. Note her ominously prophetic remark that the valentine would be 'death' to Boldwood.

Boldwood's curse

Boldwood's curse is also prophetic. His vow to take revenge on Troy creates a new element of suspense. It will eventually lead to the destruction of them both. You should note that, at this stage, Bathsheba and Boldwood find the passionate, revengeful state of his emotions equally frightening.

'This guideless woman'

Again nature mirrors man: the situation in which Bathsheba finds herself ('this guideless woman'), finds its reflection in the 'indecisive and palpitating stars'. There is a hint of things to come when we are told that Bathsheba's 'troubled spirit was far away with Troy'.

Chapter 32

Noises in the night suggest someone is stealing a horse. Gabriel and a fellow-worker pursue the thief on horses borrowed from Boldwood. The thief is revealed as Bathsheba herself, who has decided on impulse to go to Troy in Bath. She sends her workers home. It is Bathsheba's intention to warn Troy of Boldwood's desire for revenge and then never to see him again.

The pursuit

The devotion of Gabriel Oak to Bathsheba's interests is shared by Jan Coggan,

though for rather different motives. The adventures of following clues in a cross-country chase is entertaining for the reader who has the advantage on Gabriel and Jan of knowing something of Bathsheba's thoughts. The excitement of discovery is less of a surprise to the reader than to the pursuers. Examine Bathsheba's and Gabriel's reactions to this unexpected night meeting.

Bathsheba determines to meet Troy again

Bathsheba can see quite clearly what a relationship with Troy would mean for her, but her determination to be rid of him is undermined by her infatuation with him.

Chapter 33

Bathsheba is away from the farm for a week and then sends a note to say she will return after a few more days. Another week passes. News is brought by Cain,

Gabriel's assistant who has been in Bath, that Bathsheba and Troy have been seen walking arm-in-arm. Oak says nothing, but is upset by this news.

News of Troy and Bathsheba

The heat and oppressiveness, the 'monochromatic' sky and trembling air combine to create an unsettled atmosphere at the farm, in preparation for the story which follows.

In another scene involving the rustics, suspense is created while Cain slowly and painfully relates what he saw in Bath. The broken key, a recognised omen of bad luck, is an appropriate introduction to Cain's story.

Cain Ball's narrative is a deservedly famous example of Hardy's use of detail to create humour and atmosphere. First of all he is seen racing across the field, whilst the harvesters comment philosophically on his condition. Notice how more details come into view all the time, like a scene in a film. His story is dogged by physical impediments and the need for all those present to provide their own running commentaries. His version of Bath life is delightfully naive as he brings news of the great world outside Weatherbury. How does Gabriel Oak's reaction to the confused narrative differ from that of the other harvesters?

Nature and rural life

Rural life

An excellent example of Hardy's ability to fuse the comic and the significant, the realistic and the caricatured. Details are so finely chosen that we accept exaggeration; rustic comedy builds suspense and is the setting for essential information in the role of Chorus.

Gabriel's hopes would seem to have been completely dashed by Cain's news. Do you believe him when he agrees with Coggan that it really doesn't matter whose sweetheart Bathsheba is, if she can't be his?

Chapter 34

Bathsheba returns. Boldwood calls on her to apologise for his behaviour, knowing nothing of Bathsheba's visit to Bath. Boldwood meets Troy and tries to bribe him to leave Bathsheba alone and to marry Fanny. When Bathsheba comes looking for Troy, Boldwood is tormented by grief and anger at their intimacy. He again offers Troy money, this time to marry Bathsheba in order to keep her good name. Troy discloses to Boldwood that he and Bathsheba have been married in Bath, then throws the money on the ground. Boldwood resorts to threats once more and spends the night tramping the hills, alone.

A confrontation

In this extended night-scene, the paths of Bathsheba and all three of her lovers meet and cross each other. There is a mystery about Bathsheba and Troy which Boldwood, disastrously, attempts to solve.

The confrontation between Troy and Boldwood shows Boldwood's frantic desperation. Earlier, it might have seemed that his 'love' for Bathsheba had arisen more from the wish to satisfy his own desires than from any really deep and abiding love for her. However, his reaction to the news of her marriage to Troy shows a real concern for Bathsheba's welfare. Troy's callousness, which was suggested by his treatment of Fanny, is here made clear in the way he cruelly baits Boldwood. Troy deceives Boldwood by a series of lies and half-truths: Bathsheba's reputation will be ruined, she will be regarded as a 'fallen woman' if he does not marry her. He is already responsible for one destroyed reputation, of course. What is his motive in taking Boldwood's money, then throwing it in the road? Does Boldwood's concern for Bathsheba make his actions seem reasonable?

Troy's true love?

Troy's statement 'I like Fanny best' will, in retrospect, be shown to be true. Note how he goes on to replace 'like' with 'love'. His assessment of the situation is accurate when he comments that 'Miss Everdene inflamed me, and displaced Fanny for a time'. Boldwood's words, 'I've a mind to kill you' foreshadow later events again.

Troy

Love/Independent woman

Bathsheba, as we learn later, has given up her independence half-voluntarily: she boldly pursued Troy to Bath, but was driven by him into marriage. In any case, forces she cannot control are unleashed: love now leads to sadistic cruelty and threats of murder.

Chapter 35

The next morning Troy appears at an upper window of Bathsheba's house and speaks to Gabriel and Coggan. They realise that he must have married their mistress, Bathsheba. Gabriel is very upset, knowing that this hasty marriage will cause suffering to Bathsheba in the end. He resolves to hide his feelings for her sake. When Boldwood appears, his face, in contrast to Gabriel's, openly expresses anguish and appalling sorrow.

Reactions to Bathsheba's marriage

Gabriel's reaction to the unmistakeable evidence of Bathsheba's and Troy's marriage gives insight into the depth of his feelings, but he decides to be patient, so as not to cause pain to the woman he loves. Compare his reaction with Boldwood's. Read to the end of the chapter and look out for hints which Hardy gives about Boldwood's eventual tragedy.

Troy is 'out of tune'

Troy's first thoughts are directed at changing the appearance of the farmhouse. He does not 'belong' to the country in the same way as Bathsheba, Gabriel and the rustics. His ways are alien to theirs, and are out of tune with nature.

Chapter 36

At the end of August there is a harvest celebration at the farm. Troy is now master, but he is irresponsible. Gabriel knows a storm is on the way and warns Troy that the ricks should be covered. Troy takes no notice, orders brandy to be given to the farm workers and sends their women to bed. On his way home, Gabriel sees that he must cover the ricks himself if they are not to be ruined. There is no one sober enough to help, so he has to work alone.

Troy's 'gift' to the farm

The approaching storm highlights the sharp contrast between Troy and Gabriel. Gabriel, always sensitive to nature, is acutely aware of the approaching danger and the need to secure the exposed ricks, which represent the wealth of the farm. Troy, ignorant of country lore and unconcerned about the potential danger, ignores Gabriel's advice.

How does Troy show his enjoyment of the power of his new status as master? In the previous chapter he suggested changes that would need to be made at the farmhouse, and now, despite Bathsheba's misgivings, he encourages the farm workers to get drunk. His irresponsible insistence that drink should 'be the bond of their union' is in striking contrast to the sort of relations that Bathsheba tried to foster when she first took over the farm.

Instability – in nature and in women

The comment: 'Every voice in nature was unanimous in bespeaking change', and the indications noted in the previous chapter of nature 'gathering her forces' for an onslaught on the farm, now find their justification. What is

Nature and rural life

suggested about Bathsheba's changed role when she leaves the barn with the other women?

How accurate is the suggestion that the wheat is in danger because of the 'instability of woman'? Is 'instability' characteristic of Bathsheba? Note Gabriel's reaction. In tune with nature, and clear-headed about his love for Bathsheba, he is determined to save the ricks, and Bathsheba's fortune – despite Troy.

Chapter 37

Alone, Gabriel is struggling to cover the ricks when Bathsheba arrives on the scene. She is immediately grateful to Gabriel and bitterly disappointed that Troy has let both herself and the farm down so badly. Bathsheba clearly realises her husband is not the man she thought him to be. She confides in Gabriel that she married Troy because he made her jealous. Bathsheba goes back to the house, deeply grateful to Gabriel for his loyalty and dependability.

Bathsheba and Gabriel – the ricks are saved

This is another of the great natural scenes, and again Bathsheba and Gabriel are set apart from the other characters of the novel. Notice how the lightning throws their shadows over everything. As their shadows grow, they seem to grow as characters, with Bathsheba coming face-to-face with the realities of her marriage to Troy.

Examiner's tip

Hardy's control of these great set-piece scenes is remarkable. In this case, look at the almost cinematic presentation of events, but also how he uses moments of crisis to define characters and examine his recurrent theme of **Love**.

Gabriel's description of Bathsheba as 'the only venturesome' woman in the parish indicates the deep regard he still has for her, and says something about her independent spirit. Although rash decisions have brought her distress, her determined spirit will enable her to overcome it.

'between jealousy and distraction, I married him!'

Note the quiet and determined way in which Bathsheba gains Gabriel's undivided attention. After the angry vigour of the storm, it is as if a new element has entered Bathsheba's life. She is willing to admit her faults, saying that 'jealousy and distraction' prompted her to marry Troy. Her gratitude for Gabriel's devotion indicates that perhaps at last she is beginning to appreciate his sterling qualities. This is a strangely intimate scene, given the situation and the never-ending toil. You should consider why this is so: apart from other things, look at the chapter title.

This is one of a number of occasions where Bathsheba and Gabriel face nature, the elements or disaster together:

Bathsheba saves Gabriel from suffocation;
Gabriel saves Bathsheba's ricks from fire;
Gabriel saves Bathsheba's flock of sheep from death;
Bathsheba and Gabriel work in harmony, shearing sheep;
Gabriel, with Bathsheba's help, saves the ricks from the storm.

Chapter 38

As the rain pours down, the drunken men wake and go to their homes. As Gabriel walks home, he meets Boldwood. Boldwood, too, failed to cover his ricks and they have been ruined in the storm. He tells Gabriel the extent of his misery over Bathsheba, and how he wishes the locals to believe that there was never an engagement because he fears their mockery.

Contrasting characters and attitudes

Eight months previously, Gabriel had been engaged in a desperate battle to save the ricks from fire. This time, the elements threatened them with water. Previously Bathsheba was an onlooker, but this time she works with Gabriel.

Gabriel, like his name, Oak, is not overpowered by the storm. The fact that Troy walks past the ricks indifferent to their fate is perhaps not surprising, but that the rustics should do the same shows how much Troy's presence has disrupted the even tenor of their lives. Similarly, Boldwood's negligence shows his mental disintegration.

There is an element of pathos in Boldwood now. Compare the strong, silent individual that Bathsheba first saw at the Corn Exchange with this broken man, confiding his grief to Gabriel. Note also the contrast between Gabriel's love for Bathsheba and Boldwood's. Gabriel's is clear-sighted, fully aware of her weaknesses and strengths, whilst Boldwood's is warped, concentrating on his public shame and his personal grief.

Chapter 39

It is October, and Bathsheba and Troy are coming home from the market at Casterbridge. Troy has been losing money at the races, and when Bathsheba reproaches him, he tells her she has lost all her spirit. They pass a young woman on the road. It is Fanny, but Bathsheba is unaware of her identity. Fanny collapses on hearing Troy's voice. He sends Bathsheba ahead and says he will assist the woman. Troy then does what he can for Fanny; he gives her the little money he has left and arranges to meet her the following Monday morning. When he returns to Bathsheba he admits to knowing the young woman, but not by name.

Signs of disagreement

There are signs of a growing rift between Bathsheba and Troy, symbolised in their physical separation as they travel uphill, and shown in Bathsheba's listlessness contrasted with the 'erect, well-made young man'. Troy's cruelty to his horse indicates the casually vicious streak in his personality. His irresponsible use of Bathsheba's money for gambling bodes ill for the future. However, the 'flash of indignation' from Bathsheba, when Troy calls her 'a chicken-hearted creature', shows she is not completely bowed.

Troy

Love/Examiner's tip

Fanny Robin's story recurs throughout the novel, not only sad in its own right, but defining the attitudes of all the four main characters: remember Boldwood's early concern for her. Another cinematic scene of huge importance in revealing three manifestations of love.

Fanny returns

The shadowy figure of Fanny, absent from the action for a time, reappears at a crucial moment in Bathsheba's and Troy's relationship. A little while ago, Bathsheba suggested to Gabriel that she would end up in the workhouse. Fanny's appearance is a living testimony to the thoughtlessness and selfishness of Troy. His irresponsibility could lead to Bathsheba's words being fulfilled, not for herself, but for Fanny.

Troy's reaction to Fanny should be carefully noted. Later he is to claim that she is the one he really loved and you can find examples of more tender and more genuine behaviour in his short scene with her than in his scenes with Bathsheba. On the other hand, he does not do enough to save her life: what could he have done to help her survive?

Chapter 40

Fanny struggles to walk the last miles into Casterbridge to the workhouse. Her only helper is a large dog who supports her agonised steps. At the workhouse door, the dog is stoned away.

'Shutting out every speck of heaven'

The dark, moonless night, with cloud 'shutting out every speck of heaven', is a fitting setting for Fanny's hopeless situation. This scene touches the depths

Nature and rural life

of human suffering. Nature seems to provide Fanny's funeral bell: 'that acme and sublimation of all dismal sounds, the bark of a fox'. At the end, Fanny listens for human sounds – only to avoid them. With cruel irony, the only living thing to help Fanny, the dog, is stoned away from the workhouse door.

Chapter 41

Bathsheba and Troy quarrel openly and both express regret for marrying. Troy complains of having no money and Bathsheba is jealous of his feelings for the unknown beautiful woman who owned the lock of hair – not Bathsheba's – in Troy's watchcase. Bathsheba regrets having given up her freedom so hastily. On Monday news is brought that Fanny Robin is dead. Bathsheba sends Poorgrass, a farm worker, to collect her body. Bathsheba makes enquiries and learns that Fanny had been following her lover – a soldier in Troy's regiment – and that her hair was golden, the colour of the lock in Troy's watchcase.

'Bathsheba's pride... brought low'

Troy lies to Bathsheba about money and about Fanny, justifying the description of his character given in Chapter 25. For

Troy

Bathsheba, her plea to Troy: 'This is all I get...' indicates her misery. Is there now any trace left of the vanity which was characteristic of Bathsheba at the beginning of the novel? Ironically, neither she nor Troy yet appreciate the prophetic nature of his words 'women will be the death of me'.

Troy attempts to destroy Bathsheba's independence: you can no doubt find examples where her relationship with Gabriel has the opposite effect. One result of marrying Troy is that she almost immediately loses all love and respect for him. The resolution of her relationships with the three men comes nearer now that she at least has a clearer understanding of her own feelings. Note that, even though her enquiries suggest who Fanny's lover was, Bathsheba acts with humanity towards her: funeral arrangements, etc. Does Bathsheba have any fellow-feeling for Fanny, and, if so, why?

■ Self-test questions Chapters 29–41

Uncover the plot

Delete two of the three alternatives given, to find the correct plot. Beware the possible misconceptions and muddles.

Gabriel speaks to Fanny/Bathsheba/Liddy about her infatuation with Troy; she breaks off the meeting because she is meeting her lover/is in a hurry/is furious with him. She writes to refuse Boldwood – he is violently upset and threatens to harm Oak/Troy/her. She follows Troy to Bath/Casterbridge/Weatherbury and when she returns, has married him. Bathsheba/Troy/Oak and Boldwood confront each other and Boldwood is humiliated. On the night of the sheep shearing/haymaking/ harvest supper, Gabriel worries about a coming storm/hurricane/flood, but Troy dismisses his anxieties and encourages the workers to drink heavily. They all become ill/start a riot/fall asleep. Gabriel alone works to cover/move/dismantle the wheatstacks, helped by Boldwood/Bathsheba/Troy. Boldwood's ricks are ruined/only damp/saved. Bathsheba and Troy quarrel over his drinking/womanising/gambling and meet Fanny/Liddy/Maryann on the road. Troy arranges to bring her money in Weatherbury/Casterbridge/Bath and she struggles to complete the journey there. News is brought of her death by Mark Clark/Jan Coggan/Joseph Poorgrass and a hearse/wagon/carriage is sent to fetch her body.

Who? What? Why? When? Where? How?
1 Who sees Bathsheba and Troy in Bath together?
2 Whom do Bathsheba and Troy meet on the road between Casterbridge and Weatherbury?
3 What does Troy keep in the back of his watch?
4 What does Troy do with Boldwood's money?
5 Why are Bathsheba's workers unable to help Gabriel save the harvest?
6 Why does Bathsheba marry Troy, according to what she tells Gabriel?
7 When does Bathsheba begin to suspect the truth about the relationship between Troy and Fanny?
8 Where does Boldwood confront Bathsheba about her refusal to marry him?
9 How is Fanny able finally to reach the Casterbridge Union?
10 How does Troy convince Boldwood that he and Bathsheba are married?

Who says this?
1 '…don't suppose I'm content to be a nobody. I was made for better things.'
2 'Upon my heart, women will be the death of me!'
3 'loving is a misery for women always. I shall never forgive God for making me a woman, and dearly am I beginning to pay for the honour of owning a pretty face.'

Gossip, rumour and report are very important in this part of the novel. Who says this, and of whom?
1 'And they sat there together for more than half an hour, talking moving things, and she once was crying a'most to death. And when they came out, her eyes were shining and she was as white as a lily;…'
2 'She was such a limber maid that 'a could stand no hardship, even when I knowed her, and 'a went like a candle-snuff, so 'tis said.'
3 'Where is he gone? He helped me.'
4 'I believe him to have no conscience at all.'
5 'I do feel a little regret occasionally, but no woman ever had power over me for any length of time.'
6 'I once heard than an uncle of his was queer in his head, but I don't know the rights o't.'

Prove it!
Find a quote from the text that could be used to back up each of the following statements. (The numbers in brackets refer to the chapter you might like to look up in the commentary for help.)
1 Bathsheba loses the control over herself and events that she has had in general throughout the novel when she falls in love with Troy (29)
2 Troy tells lies when it suits him (29)

Chapter 42

Fanny's coffin is collected from the workhouse by Poorgrass. On the way back to the farm he stops at the Buck's Head Inn, where he has too much to drink. Gabriel finds him and drives the wagon and its sad burden home. The delay means it is too late for the funeral to be held that day and Bathsheba orders the coffin to be brought into the house for the night. Gabriel, in order to spare Bathsheba's feelings, rubs out the words 'and child' from the names marked on the coffin.

A funeral delayed

Nature reflects the sadness of the occasion. The sky is closed in by 'dark spongy

forms', and the first fog of autumn draws down upon the wagon. Joseph Poorgrass' detour via the inn delays the funeral and creates enough time for Bathsheba to learn the truth.

It is a little while since there was an interlude in the narrative for the rustics to play their part. Now they comment

Nature and rural life

on Fanny's death and give their views on religious practices. This humorous interlude provides relief in a situation which is becoming melodramatic.

Once again the appearance of the rustics combines comedy and serious purpose. The timidity of Joseph Poorgrass, the old-fashioned ways of the inn, the solemnly inane discussion are amusing and there is outrageous black humour in their drinking and singing while the coffin waits outside. More seriously, even tragically, how does the scene reflect Fanny's life?

Rural life

A beautifully-judged scene of rustic tragi-comedy. Visually memorable (Poorgrass's journey, the coffin outside the inn) and full of comic dialogue, it is a final example of how the world has treated Fanny and a hint of the unnatural: soon the coffin will be opened.

Chapter 43

As Bathsheba sits up waiting for Troy to come home, Liddy tells her of the rumour in the village – that Fanny died having a child. Bathsheba goes to visit Gabriel, hoping for advice, but then changes her mind and returns home. She unscrews the coffin and sees Fanny and her baby for herself. She kneels in prayer, then, though distraught with grief and jealousy, puts flowers inside the coffin. Troy arrives and, full of remorse, kisses the dead Fanny. Then he turns on Bathsheba. In despair, Bathsheba runs from the house.

'a further misgiving'

Has Bathsheba had some strange premonition about the coffin that she should now suffer the 'gravity of a further misgiving'? We may guess the content of the rumour which Liddy whispers in her ear by the agitated manner of her response and her comment that there is 'only one name' written on the coffin cover.

A desire to 'speak to some one stronger'

Bathsheba is finally coming to appreciate the strength of Gabriel's steadfastness and to recognise both the weakness of her own self-regard and the shallowness of Boldwood's love compared with Gabriel's unselfishness.

Events have come full circle. There was a time when Gabriel stood outside a window looking in on Bathsheba. Now it is Bathsheba's turn to be the wanderer in the night, watching Gabriel by his fireside. Note her envy of the 'atmosphere of content' which seems to emanate from Gabriel's home, in contrast to her own household.

Bathsheba's state of mind after opening the coffin terrifies her so much that she grasps at the image of Gabriel at prayer to help her retain sanity. Like him, she kneels and prays. Despite their physical separation, at this moment she and Gabriel are closer than they have ever been.

Bathsheba is rejected

There is a rare moment of tenderness from Troy when he kisses Fanny and

it marks the end of his relationship with Bathsheba. The extent of Bathsheba's emotional turmoil is demonstrated in her wild scene before Fanny's coffin.

Troy's brutal insensitivity to Bathsheba's suffering is shown by his words to the dead Fanny: 'but never mind… you are my very, very wife!'

Chapter 44

Bathsheba spends the night in a wood. In the early morning, Liddy finds her and persuades her to return to the house, since Troy has gone out and the coffin is about to be moved to the churchyard. Once the coffin has gone, Bathsheba goes into the house and stays in the attic. Liddy informs her that a splendid tombstone marks Fanny's grave.

Bathsheba is distraught, but not despairing. After a night hiding in a thicket, she faces the day with 'a cooler brain' and is delighted at the approach of Liddy Smallbury. In particular, when she and Liddy barricade themselves in the attic, there are signs of a more positive approach: though she at first chooses books to suit her gloomy mood, she has no intention of being bored and settles for lighter reading.

At the end of the chapter notice the ominous colour of the 'blood-red' sun. Nature seems to be warning that the drama is not yet over.

Chapter 45

Hardy describes what Troy did and thought after Bathsheba ran away. He replaced the lid on the coffin, spent a sleepless night, collected all the money he could and went to Casterbridge, where he ordered a magnificent tombstone for Fanny. Later, in the evening, he planted flowers on Fanny's grave by the light of a lantern. It began to rain and Troy sheltered in the church porch, where he fell asleep.

A flashback

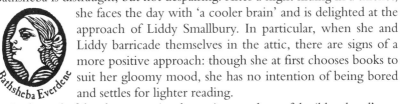

The flashback to events before Troy learns of Fanny's death provides the explanation for his absence. Troy went to keep his appointment with Fanny on the Monday morning, as arranged. His irritation, when she did not arrive, drove away concern for her. It was not until much later that he realised something must have happened to her.

Troy

Money for a headstone

The way in which Troy uses the money intended for Fanny is both ironic and typical of his character. His expression of his love is showy and dramatic, but Fanny's death has been brought about by his failure to express his love in more practical ways: marital and financial. His pointless flower planting and his naming of himself on the tomb (revealed in the next chapter) reflect the same character. Why do you think he named himself as the donor: love, vanity, desire to hurt Bathsheba?

Love

You should be asking questions about Troy's love at this stage. Is his protestation of love for Fanny genuine? If so, why did he treat her like he did? What motivates his elaborate tributes? It is not easy to find much to admire in Troy, but he is not unfeeling.

Chapter 46

During the night, rainwater runs down from the church roof onto Fanny's grave, washing away the flowers Troy has planted. The next day, Troy finds the grave ruined, and leaves in despair. Bathsheba and Gabriel, who have gone separately to visit Fanny's grave, meet there and set about replanting the flowers and repairing the damage.

Troy departs

Troy

If Troy had left the scene immediately after planting the flowers, he could have gone away satisfied that he had left a lasting and beautiful remembrance of his love for Fanny. But having slept the night in the church porch, he is there in the morning to witness the devastation of his efforts. Note how swiftly he gives up the struggle and leaves the village on the Budmouth road.

Bathsheba cares for Fanny's grave

Bathsheba Everdene

In the final paragraph of the chapter, we see Bathsheba's developing maturity as she tidies Fanny's grave and issues instructions to ensure it remains in good condition. She is now in control of herself and her emotions.

Chapter 47

Troy arrives at the coast at Budmouth. He intends to take a swim but is carried out to sea by the tide. A passing ship picks him up.

Troy's removal from Weatherbury and his presumed death allow the story to move to a climax, with Boldwood once more coming to the fore in Bathsheba's life. Is it all too convenient and coincidental? Certainly it seems slightly contrived, but you will note that Troy's emotional state is likely to lead to thoughtless acts. Hardy cleverly gives the reader half the truth: we know that the belief in his death is wrong, we guess that he will probably return, but we have no idea of how or where he is spending his time.

Chapter 48

As the days pass, Bathsheba realises that she is in danger of losing her farm if Troy is unable to pay the rent. He has not returned. At the market she is informed that Troy has been drowned. Bathsheba denies the truth of this but still faints with shock. Boldwood is present and catches her as she falls. Bathsheba returns home. At first she doubts the truth of the reports of Troy's death, but later begins to think they might be true.

Fate places Boldwood on the spot to assist Bathsheba when she faints at the news of Troy's drowning. But Bathsheba, even in her distraught state, has sufficient presence of mind to decline his offer to take her home.

The final paragraph of this chapter marks the turning-point in Bathsheba's transition from girl to mature woman: whilst she accepts that she no longer has any part in Troy, she still finds it in herself to keep the lock of Fanny's hair in remembrance of her.

Chapter 49

Almost a year passes. Gabriel is made farm bailiff. He also looks after Boldwood's lower farm. Gabriel's fortunes rise, but he still lives a simple life. Boldwood hopes to persuade Bathsheba to marry him. He is prepared to wait: legally she will be free to remarry seven years after her husband's disappearance.

The seasons denote the passage of time during which Gabriel's status grows, Bathsheba lives quietly, and Boldwood resumes his hopes of winning her hand. The stability described is pleasant, after previous drama, but Boldwood is still as obsessive and the last paragraph hints at the occasion which will disturb the barely established peace: Greenhill Fair.

Chapter 50

Bathsheba and Boldwood take their flocks to Greenhill Sheep Fair. Gabriel and Cain Ball attend. There are entertainments at the fair. Troy reappears, now a circus performer playing the role of Dick Turpin. We are told something of his recent life. Bathsheba watches his performance without recognising him, but Pennyways, her former bailiff, does and gives her a note to inform her. While she is talking to Boldwood, Troy manages to snatch the note before she has read it.

A dashing thief

Hardy's description of the sheep fair is vivid and realistic. Its animation and bustle is in contrast to the recent inaction. However Troy's reappearance at the fair sets the plot in motion again.

It is fitting that Troy should play the part of Turpin – a well-known and dashing villain. It is also prophetic that he plays a part which ends in his being shot. He has lost none of his vanity, for his embarrassment is not merely lest he should be discovered, but that he should be discovered to have fallen so low. Nonetheless, his audacious theft of Pennyways' note suggests that his character has not changed during his absence.

A dramatic scene

Hardy uses every possible method to build up the drama associated with Turpin's Ride, both the spectacle itself and events around it. Drums and trumpets, pushing crowds (including the innocently wondering Poorgrass and Coggan), build up to the appearance of Sergeant Troy. How is the off-stage drama increased by Boldwood's seating arrangements for Bathsheba and that on-stage by Troy's sighting of her? Boldwood and Bathsheba's respectable tea-drinking is broken into by the highly visual scene where Troy boldly steals the note from Pennyways.

Chapter 51

On the journey home from the fair, Boldwood rides his horse beside Bathsheba's gig. He asks her again about marriage. She promises to give him a decision by Christmas. Some weeks pass. Bathsheba talks to Gabriel, who gives her sensible advice, but he says nothing of his love for her.

Bathsheba – another problem with Boldwood

Bathsheba's remorse for the anguish she has caused Boldwood makes her express her pity for him too freely. Boldwood is sufficiently encouraged to ask: 'would you repair the old wrong to me by marrying me?' Given her past experience, her answer should have been unequivocal. Has she still not discovered the difference between pity, infatuation, and love? In this long discussion, can she not see a reprise of previous conversations with Boldwood?

Bathsheba's talk with Gabriel concerning the 'toil' she finds herself in again with Boldwood indicates the trust she now has in Gabriel, but also shows insensitivity to his feelings. At the end of the chapter she feels disappointed that he has not regarded her feelings: he should have hinted that he would wait for her like Boldwood. Is Bathsheba's disappointment justified?

Look back to Chapter 4 to see how Bathsheba's views on love have changed. There is something mildly insulting to Gabriel in her concern that she has hurt Boldwood deeply.

This latest approach from Boldwood, and Bathsheba's continuing inability to recognise and value Gabriel's love, are both strong reminders of events before Troy came on the scene. Troy's first appearance led to a quickening of the action: Bathsheba discovered a lot about herself and about him, Boldwood's unbalanced state began to show, whilst Gabriel's steadfastness and reliability were demonstrated. Troy's relationship with Fanny came to light, with the resulting deflation of Bathsheba's vanity and the end of her fragile happiness with Troy. Troy's return signals that events are to be set in motion again.

Chapter 52

Boldwood is to give a Christmas party. Bathsheba feels that she is the undeclared 'guest of honour' and this makes her uncomfortable. Boldwood looks forward cheerfully to the event. In Casterbridge, Troy and Pennyways make plans. Troy will confront Bathsheba. His main concern is to secure his share of her money and property, not to return to her.

A meeting prepared for

Note how Hardy has constructed this chapter. It is divided into seven short sections, each dealing with a different strand of the plot. The first section sets the scene for the coming action and, in spite of the revelry, 'a shadow seemed to move about the rooms'. The omens for the party are not good.

The title, 'Converging Courses', implies that something dramatic or tragic will result when the three people meet. Note how carefully Hardy patterns the various sections. After the introduction, the other six sections follow Bathsheba, Boldwood and Troy in sequence. Look at the opening words of Sections 2, 3 and 4 and the opening sentences of Sections 5, 6 and 7 to see how Hardy wants us to be aware of this pattern and therefore of the approaching menace.

Bathsheba is uneasy

Despite sitting at her mirror, Bathsheba is no longer prey to the vanity which would formerly have dominated her thoughts. She is uneasy about attending the party. Does her black dress symbolise her expectation of a joyless future?

Boldwood puts his affairs in order

Notice how choosy Boldwood is now about his dress. His hands shake and he cannot tie his neckerchief: he is clearly agitated. Note the way that Boldwood seems to be putting his affairs in order. This is ironic because he does so in anticipation of marrying Bathsheba. In fact, his future will be very different.

Chapter 53

The rustics have heard rumours that Troy is in Casterbridge but they fight shy of going to the party to tell Bathsheba. Troy eavesdrops on a discussion about Boldwood's obsession with Bathsheba. At the party, Bathsheba prepares to leave early. Boldwood seeks her out and persuades her to agree to marry him at the end of six years, if Troy has not returned. He gives her a ring. Just as Bathsheba is leaving, Troy appears to claim her. Boldwood takes a gun and shoots him. He is restrained from killing himself and, leaving the house, walks out into the night.

The rustics have their say

Nature and rural life

Before the events of the party unfold, the rustics voice their opinions about the possible effect of Troy's return and the trouble he has already caused to the folk of Weatherbury. This part of the chapter builds up tension, with the rustics' shock at Boldwood's continuing 'fancy', the 'turn' that seeing Troy's face gave them and Laban Tall's failed attempt to give warning to Bathsheba.

The climax of the plot

The title of the chapter tells us that, when the courses mentioned in Chapter 52 run together, the climax will follow instantly. Why should Hardy decide to express this in Latin? You will notice how brief this confrontation is: Hardy has prepared it so thoroughly that no more is needed. Events escalate from Bathsheba's attempts to refuse Boldwood. From her submission and his contentment progress is rapid. The men try to tell Bathsheba, to be interrupted by Troy's rapping at the door. Boldwood welcomes him until his 'mechanical laugh' reveals his identity. Troy summons Bathsheba and Boldwood (in 'thin tones', 'as if from a dungeon') says she must go with Troy. She resists, Troy seizes her, she screams, a shot rings out. In terms of the text, it is less than a page since Boldwood recognised Troy. How does this bewilderingly rapid sequence heighten the drama?

Examiner's tip

Hardy writes most convincingly of character, though his style can be clumsy. For these reasons his structural skill tends to be neglected. In an examination you should be able to show how dramatically the climax is plotted: masterly use of the omniscient narrator with an ever-shifting viewpoint.

Chapter 54

Boldwood walks into Casterbridge gaol and gives himself up. In Boldwood's hall, Bathsheba holds Troy's body in her arms and sends Gabriel to find a doctor. When the surgeon arrives, he finds that Bathsheba has left. She has had Troy's body taken home where, refusing help, she has laid him out in preparation for burial. Bathsheba then collapses and Liddy hears her mistress pass the night in self-recrimination and misery.

Bathsheba fulfils her duty

Bathsheba moves instinctively to take Troy in her arms. Her response to his murder is full of dignity, strength, courage, and tenderness, showing how much she has changed from the vain girl at the beginning of the novel. She shows 'the heart of a wife' in taking sole responsibility for laying out her dead husband. She also recognises her guilt in initiating the events that led to the tragedy: acceptance of guilt is a sign of maturity, as is the fact that she soon abandons the suicidal impulses she now feels: 'how can I live!'. Notice how the pace of the novel slows again after the drama of the previous chapter.

Chapter 55

Boldwood is sent for trial the following March. There is evidence of his mental instability. His obsessive desire to have Bathsheba as his wife is revealed when a hoard of jewels and expensive clothes is found in a locked room in his house. These are all labelled with the name Bathsheba Boldwood. Though Boldwood pleads guilty and the death sentence is passed, the local people petition the Home Secretary to change the sentence to life imprisonment. They are successful.

Bathsheba Boldwood

Note the 'pathetic evidences' in Boldwood's house of 'a mind crazed with care and love'. Only now do we begin to appreciate the depth of Boldwood's obsessive love for Bathsheba and the enormity of the tragedy which her single act of thoughtlessness brought about.

Time passes

At the beginning of the chapter 'we pass rapidly on' some two or three months. The dramas are over: all that remains for Hardy is to find the suitable conclusion for each of his five main characters: in this chapter Boldwood, in the next Fanny and Troy, finally Bathsheba and Gabriel. Boldwood is reprieved: why do you think that Hardy decided not to extend his tragedy by execution?

Chapter 56

Bathsheba has kept to herself for months. One day she visits the churchyard where Troy and Fanny are buried together in the same grave. Oak meets her there by accident and tells her that he is planning to move to California the following spring. Throughout the autumn, Gabriel avoids seeing Bathsheba, which causes her distress. After Christmas, Gabriel's letter of resignation arrives. Bathsheba realises she cannot manage without him and goes to see him. Gabriel states frankly that he is leaving because local gossips say he is only staying in the hope that she will marry him. Eventually, Bathsheba intimates that she might, after all, be willing to marry him. Oak has not asked her since her refusal in Chapter 4.

Bathsheba finally makes up her mind

With the emergence of spring comes new hope, and Bathsheba gradually turns back to her farming concerns. Note how Bathsheba demonstrates her maturity in her choice of resting-place for Troy.

Consider how Bathsheba has changed. How does she now feel about running the farm, about people's opinion of her, and about Gabriel's plans to emigrate?

When, finally, Bathsheba seeks Gabriel out and declares her love, she is no longer the vain young girl who once rejected him. The strength and enduring quality of their love is stressed by the lack of 'pretty phrases' with which they declare it.

Chapter 57

One misty morning, Bathsheba and Gabriel marry very quietly with only two witnesses present. That evening, the villagers gather to express their goodwill. They good-naturedly refuse refreshment, but Gabriel sends food and drink to the Malthouse so that they can drink a toast. The novel ends on a note of peaceful harmony.

Suited

The dreary weather is strangely fitting for the 'most private, secret, plainest wedding' which is Bathsheba's desire. As country folk, they dress to suit both the occasion and the weather.

Nature and rural life

Fittingly, the novel ends with a few words from Joseph Poorgrass, a representative of the community to which the newly-weds belong.

At the start of the novel we would have thought that the wedding of Bathsheba and Gabriel would form an ideal happy ending. In some ways it seems as if the intervening tragedies have never happened: Bathsheba, wearing her hair as she had on Norcombe Hill, seems in Gabriel's eyes 'remarkably like the girl of that fascinating dream', but now she never laughs readily. In Chapter 55 Liddy describes her as having been 'a romping girl' when she arrived at Weatherbury. How has she changed? How does the reader now feel about the final union between her and Gabriel Oak?

Independent woman/Love

Has Bathsheba foregone her independence in marriage? Or has she found that independence and selfishness are not the same thing? Notice in the last two chapters that neither one imposes ('These two sensible people deemed…') and the **Rural** community becomes 'their' friend.

Uncover the plot
Delete two of the three alternatives given, to find the correct plot. Beware possible misconceptions and muddles.

Fanny's coffin is taken to Boldwood's/Bathsheba's/Oak's house overnight and Bathsheba opens it to find out if Fanny is beautiful/is still alive/had a child. Troy, interrupting her, is full of remorse/very angry/very upset and kisses the dead mother and child – Bathsheba cries out: "Traitor!"/"I hate you!"/"Kiss me too!" He repulses her and she faints/runs away/screams, only agreeing to return when Fanny/Troy/Liddy is taken away. Troy buys Fanny a tombstone for £500/£50/£27 and plants flowers on her grave, but rain from the roof/a gargoyle/a water barrel destroys his hard work. He leaves in despair and is thought to have been arrested/killed himself/drowned. Time passes, and Gabriel becomes shepherd/owner/bailiff of both farms; Bathsheba agrees to consider marrying him/Boldwood/Pennyways in 3/5/6 years' time. On Christmas Eve/Easter Day/New Year's Day, they become engaged but Troy returns and Boldwood stabs/shoots/strangles him. One fine/stormy/rainy day a year/three years/seven years later, Bathsheba finally marries Boldwood/Gabriel/Joseph Poorgrass.

Who? What? Why? When? Where? How?
1   Who repairs Fanny's ruined grave?
2   Who first recognises Troy when he returns?
3   What causes Boldwood to fire the shot that kills Troy?
4   What does Bathsheba do with Troy's body on the night of his death?
5   Why is Chapter 43 called 'Fanny's Revenge'?
6   Why is Troy assumed to have drowned?
7   Where does Bathsheba finally agree to marry Gabriel?
8   Where does Bathsheba bury Troy?
9   How does Bathsheba react when she first sees Troy after his return?
10 How does Gabriel try to shield Bathsheba from the truth about the dead Fanny?

Who is this?
1   'She was the stuff of which great men's mothers are made.'
2   'The one feat alone – that of dying – by which a mean condition could be resolved into a grand one, (she) had achieved.'
3   'He had not minded the peculiarities of his birth, the vicissitudes of his life, the meteor-like uncertainty of all that related to him, because these appertained to the hero of this story, without whom there would have been no story at all for him;…'
4   'He now wears shining boots with hardly a hob in 'em, two or three times a-week, and a tall hat a-Sundays…'
5   '…she never laughed readily now…'
6   'She's hot and hasty, but she's a brave girl who'll never tell a lie however much the truth may harm her…'

Who are these?
1   'He was hers and she was his; they should be gone together… I am nothing to either of them…'
2   Who suffers from 'a multiplying eye' and what is it? (42)
3   Who have 'the most private, secret, plainest wedding that it is possible to have'?

4   Who says: 'You are nothing to me – nothing… A ceremony before a priest doesn't make a marriage. I am not morally yours.'?

Parallel lines

Several events and images in the novel are echoed elsewhere; Hardy uses this device to shape and unify his story. Where do the following lines/events/images find an echo (or echoes) in the text?

1   Fanny is helped by a stray dog on her journey to Casterbridge Union. Where else does a dog affect the plot?

2   Troy is immediately recognisable in his red coat, and is identified with it. Where else do images of red make a startling effect?

3   Troy keeps a lock of Fanny's hair in his watch. Where else does a lock of hair feature?

4   'Some women only require an emergency to make them fit for one.' (7) Find a quote about Bathsheba in Chapter 54 which echoes this line.

5   Bathsheba orders Joseph to cover Fanny's funeral wagon with flowers; where else in the novel been bright with flowers?

6   When Troy's spur becomes entangled in Bathsheba's dress, there is a striking description of how their shadows are thrown by the lantern light on to the landscape. 'It radiated upwards into their faces, and sent over half the plantation gigantic shadows of both man and woman, each dusky shape becoming distorted and mangled upon the tree trunks till it wasted to nothing.' (24) A similar phenomenon is described when Bathsheba and Gabriel work to save her wheat from the storm (37). Find the quote, and say what effect these two descriptions have.

7   Gabriel and Bathsheba's love is described and differentiated from her passion for Troy and Boldwood's passion for her: 'Theirs was that substantial affection which arises… when the two who are thrown together begin first by knowing the rough sides of each other's character, and not the best till further on, the romance growing up in the interstices of a mass of hard prosaic reality.' (56) Find examples in the novel of how the two have worked together in peace and harmony.

8   Gabriel becomes an employee of Bathsheba's when he saves her property from fire (6). How many other times does he save the farm?

9   Which attempt of his to shield Bathsheba goes badly wrong?

10 It is during an evening party that Troy is killed. (53) Pick out four other events that happen at night and say what effect the time of day gives to the scenes.

How to write a coursework essay

Most of you are probably studying *Far from the Madding Crowd* as part of a Wide Reading coursework assignment for GCSE English/English Literature. If we look at the requirement of the NEAB examinations, we find that this assignment must involve *comparison* between a complete pre-twentieth-century prose text and a suitable twentieth-century text. It is also essential to make certain comments on the historical, social and cultural background to the texts. Thomas Hardy's novels are particularly suitable in this respect: his presentation of nineteenth-century rustic life is crucial to the success of his fiction. In the following pages we examine three possible subjects for Wide Reading assignments. Throughout the **Text commentary** the **Essays icon** draws attention to useful material for these assignments.

There are, of course, some general principles for these assignments. *Comparison is essential.* No credit is given for telling the story of all or part of *Far from the Madding Crowd* and that of a twentieth-century story with a vaguely similar theme. It is essential that you show that, while Hardy's presentation of love or rural society makes has a certain effect, your twentieth-century author affects the reader totally differently, in the same way or in a partially similar way.

Though comparison is essential, it is not required that you devote an equal amount of your essay to each of the texts. Similarly, there is no requirement that your twentieth-century comparative text is another novel: short stories, plays and poems are acceptable, and the only restriction is that the text 'must be of sufficient substance and quality to merit serious study'. In the case of Hardy an unusual situation arises: much of his best love poetry was written after the death of his wife in 1912 and it would be possible to deal with Hardy's treatment of love in novels and poems.

Your choice of twentieth-century comparative text is important. There must be *specific* grounds for comparison. Similarities to Hardy are not easy to find (he is a very distinctive novelist), so remember that your twentieth-century example can be different, even opposite, in effect from Hardy: using similar ideas differently is a good ground for comparison.

The *most important consideration* in writing the essay is that it must develop an argument or explain a point of view consistently throughout. Choosing a title matters: if you write an essay called 'Farm Workers in Thomas Hardy and John Steinbeck', you are not directing yourself towards a specific comparison. The comparison should be made throughout the essay, not necessarily in the same sentence, but at least in adjacent paragraphs. Careful advance planning will aid you in organising your theme or argument: making notes on the material, putting these notes in order, then working through two or three drafts of the essay. Thus you should be able to make a decision on what each paragraph is about, as far as possible signalling that to the reader in the opening sentence, often called a *topic sentence* because it states the topic of the paragraph.

In terms of length of essay, do bear in mind that it is only one of several pieces of coursework and there is no need for a 5,000 word blockbuster. Many essays will exceed 1,000 words: by how much depends on the material you wish to present and the advice of your teacher.

Rural life

How does Hardy use the characters and activities of rural life to enhance the enjoyment and significance of Far *from the Madding Crowd?*

Compare the ways in which he presents farm-life with John Steinbeck's in Of Mice and Men.

Before starting, note the paired words in the first sentence: characters *and* activities, enjoyment *and* significance. All need to be dealt with. You may well be studying *Of Mice and Men* for your examination, but there are other suitable choices for comparison: Fred Kitchen's *Brother to the Ox*, for instance, or, with a slight change of title, many of the stories or novels of D.H. Lawrence (who provides a good comparison with Hardy on several topics).

Both *Far from the Madding Crowd* and *Of Mice and Men* present their central relationship(s) against a background of agricultural activity: in the case of *Far from the Madding Crowd*, the relationships are much more complicated, but, though it is something like five times the length of *Of Mice and Men* and has totally different narrative goals, the use of rural activities is comparable. Hardy sets many important scenes against a background of the farm-year (shearing, harvest, etc) or agricultural disasters (swollen sheep or endangered ricks); Steinbeck's narrative never leaves the ranch (except for the opening and closing sections), and bucking barley, raising pups and setting up a farm are essential to the story. You should not find it difficult to explain the importance of farm activities in both books: for instance, Gabriel's reliability and Boldwood's emotional collapse are both shown in their response to the great storm; the characters of George and Lennie are expressed through their dream of their own farm. You will find Hardy more entertaining in his presentation of these activities: perhaps his descriptions could be described as 'colourful', Steinbeck's as 'harsh'. Both are more or less realistic, but Hardy is writing of the recent past with some nostalgia, Steinbeck of the present in a mood of social criticism.

Hardy's rustic characters provide a source of humour and fulfil a choric function: that is to say, they act like the Chorus in a Greek tragedy, telling of events the reader has not witnessed, commenting on characters and warning of what is to come. There is something of this role in the bunk-house characters in *Of Mice and Men*, but the greatest similarity you will find is the creation of a set of contrasted characters within a common group, mostly uneducated and with more than their share of inadequates and eccentrics. The difference is that Hardy's characters are often treated humorously, Steinbeck's only occasionally, but comparisons can be made between, say, Joseph Poorgrass and Candy, the sweeper. You should have no difficulty proving that both novels contain a varied selection of farm/ranch workers who sometimes influence the plot and frequently comment on it.

You should also make sure that you include comments on the differences in the rural setting: 100 years of time and many thousands of miles. This could, in fact, be well used in either an introductory or concluding section. You should also take note of such similarities as the theatricality of parts of *Far from the Madding Crowd* and all of *Of Mice and Men*, notably the extent to which dialogue creates character.

The independent woman

Bathsheba Everdene attempts an independence of action and decision that is unusual in Victorian fiction. How far are her situation and her perception of herself similar to those of a modern would-be liberated female character, like Marian in Margaret Atwood's The Edible Woman?

With this particular title it is necessary to begin with a section on Bathsheba before beginning the comparison. You might like to examine her search for independence in two areas: business and marriage. In love and marriage she is independent, admitting no outside influence and virtually proposing to Gabriel at the end, having unceremoniously refused him at the beginning. She makes many wrong decisions, such as luring Boldwood with the valentine, but so do the men and Bathsheba has the excuse of youth. Only in the marriage to Troy does she lose her independence, shown in such instances as leaving the barn at the harvest supper and fleeing the house on the night before Fanny's funeral, but even here things are not simple. It is partly her independence (riding to Bath) that causes her problems and she speedily banishes the fears that drive her into the wood.

In business there is a definite sense that an independent woman cannot cope on her own: you will have no difficulty finding examples where Gabriel has to rescue her property and in Chapter 29 he refuses to be dismissed by her because she needs him. The predictions that a young woman cannot run a farm on her own come true, but for all that you should remember the independent spirit and perception of her responsibility that prompts actions like working with Gabriel on the ricks.

How does this compare with Marian MacAlpin, one of many modern female protagonists we could have chosen? She is, to begin with, much less independent than Bathsheba, in a conventional job, keeping on the right side of a conventional landlady and never doubting her conventional boy-friend. Her progress towards independence (through spectacular drunk-scenes, eating disorders and a brief affair with a student who makes lack of commitment a way of life) leaves her with the past destroyed and nothing in its place.

You can thus make a case for Bathsheba being far more independent and liberated than Atwood's heroine. However, the essential difference is that the standards by which she is judged tend to be male standards: it is not just the workers, but Hardy himself, who comment on female weaknesses (though the story he creates reveals Bathsheba as stronger than most of the male characters). There is no omniscient (all-knowing) narrator in Atwood's book. It is a mixture of first and third person narrative, but the third person is closely allied to Marian (half her divided personality?). Bathsheba asserts her independence by what she *does*, Marian by what she *becomes*. A conventionally happy marriage would not be a suitable ending for *The Edible Woman*.

Margaret Atwood is a notably subtle and witty author and you could find many books or stories which present similar comparisons and contrasts in a more straightforward narrative.

Love

Analyse Hardy's presentation of the theme of love in Far from the Madding Crowd, *considering the various types of love he presents and the consequences it has for the characters' lives. Compare his treatment of the theme with J.B. Priestley's in* An Inspector Calls.

Far from the Madding Crowd is one of the great love stories of nineteenth-century fiction and you should certainly consider love as a possible theme for a coursework essay. Here we are looking at a fairly straightforward title. The choice of twentieth-century comparison (which, again, may be an examination text for you) is to remind you that this text need not be a novel and also that unlikely-seeming titles can provide grounds for comparison.

You should consider all five main characters, Fanny Robin included, and a useful starting point is the section on **Love** in the **Themes** section of this book.

Many of the points that you will make are obvious ones: the dashing superficiality of Troy contrasted to the dogged fanaticism of Boldwood, for instance. You should consider such matters as the differences in Bathsheba's love for the three men, which characters change and develop in their emotions, which characters are dominated by love or are victims of love and which have a more balanced outlook. Of great importance is the connection between love and violence: two deaths are in some way connected with love, as is one near-execution. Consider also which characters choose wisely in love.

The J.B. Priestley play is not a love story, but love in various aspects helps to bring about the tragedy and the characters' weaknesses are revealed in part through their relationships with the opposite sex. Interestingly enough, the closest comparison is between a character who never appears on stage in Priestley's play and a character who appears only in some five chapters of Hardy's novel. Eva Smith and Fanny Robin are both victims of love, both victims of poverty, and both have the ability to ruin their tormenters' lives from beyond the grave. *An Inspector Calls* lacks characters who show any devotion in love (or in human relationships generally) and this is part of Priestley's message: at the end of the play nobody is rewarded like Bathsheba and Gabriel with a fulfilling relationship. The young men are drab versions of Sergeant Troy, thoroughly selfish in love, with an illegitimate child taking a central position in the tragedies of Eva and Fanny. Note that Priestley can afford to be a little franker and less delicate on matters of sex than Hardy. At some stage also you should be able to write a paragraph or two on the role of class in determining attitudes to love in the two texts.

An essay on love in *Far from the Madding Crowd* could, of course, take a conventional love story of the twentieth century for comparison. This would be a perfectly sound choice, as long as you remember that by no means all romances would be regarded as being of sufficient literary worth: check with your teacher!

■ How to write an examination essay

Though most of you will be required to write on *Far from the Madding Crowd* as part of your coursework, some of you may need to answer an examination question on it. This section considers one specific title on the novel, but also gives general advice on how to approach an English Literature essay.

Several of the major events in the novel concern potentially tragic loss of Bathsheba's farm saved by Gabriel. Consider the episodes of the rick-fire, the dying sheep and the storm, commenting on the ways in which Hardy creates atmosphere and the importance of these events in revealing the central relationships of the novel.

Before you start writing

- The first essential is thorough revision. It is important that you realise that even Open Book examinations require close textual knowledge. You will have time to look up quotations and references, but *only if you know where to look.*

- Read the questions very carefully, both to choose the best one and to take note of exactly what you are asked to do.

- Do not answer the question you *imagine or hope* has been set. In the case of the title we are considering, you are not asked to tell the story of the episodes, though a brief indication of events would help. You are asked to consider the ways in which Hardy creates atmosphere: the contrasted colours and confused sights of the fire create excitement, for instance, or the semi-humorous delays of the rustics build up suspense for the swollen sheep. Also you must relate the events to the relationships of the central characters: the storm emphasises the bonds between Oak and Bathsheba, the wild irresponsibility of Troy and Boldwood's loss of will through hopeless love.

- Identify all the key words in the question that mention characters, events and themes, and instructions as to what to do, e.g. compare, contrast, comment, give an account, etc. Write a short list of the things you have to do. In this case 'consider' is a fairly open-ended term (you are to think about it and come up with your own opinion), but the two main areas of comment are clearly defined.

- Look at the points you have identified and jot down what you are going to say about each. For example, think around each episode considering all five main characters. There is no episode which involves all five, but they all appear in at least one: don't forget Fanny in the aftermath of the fire. Make notes on how the Gabriel/Bathsheba relationship changes through these episodes.

- Decide in what order you are going to deal with the main points. Number them in sequence. This is a matter of choice, but do not use chronological order: 'When Gabriel arrives in Weatherbury, he sees that there is a fire.' You may, in this case, wish to treat the three episodes in the order in which they occur in the book, but do not forget to make cross-references between them on both atmosphere and relationships.

Writing the essay

- The first sentences are important. Try to summarise your response to the question so the examiner has some idea of how you plan to approach it. For example: 'The three episodes where Gabriel Oak comes to the rescue of Bathsheba's farm provide drama with subtly varied atmosphere and suggest an increasing bond between the two characters.' Jump straight into the essay; do not nibble at the edges for a page and a half. A personal response is rewarded, but you must always answer the question – as you write your essay, *refer back* to your list of points.

- Answer *all* of the question. Many students spend all their time answering just one part of a question and ignoring the rest. This prevents you gaining marks for the parts left out. In the same way, failing to answer enough questions on the examination is a waste of marks which can always be gained most easily at the start of an answer.

- There is no 'correct' length for an essay. What you must do is to spend the full time usefully in answering all parts of the question: spending longer than the allocated time by more than a few minutes is dangerous. It is an advantage if you can organise your time so well as to reach an elegant conclusion (perhaps on the incidents as markers in the course of the love of Bathsheba and Gabriel), but it is better to leave an essay without a conclusion than to fail to start the next question.

- Take care with presentation, spelling and punctuation. It is generally unwise to use slang or contractions (e.g. 'they've' for 'they have').

- Use quotation or paraphrase when it is relevant and contributes to the quality and clarity of your answer. References to events often do not need quotation, but the exact words of, for instance, Bathsheba's messages about saving the sheep are revealing of character. *Extended* quotations are usually unhelpful and are often used as padding, which is a complete waste of time.

■ Self-test answers Chapters 1–15

Uncover the plot

Gabriel Oak observes a beautiful girl and particularly notices her vanity. Later, she refuses his proposal of marriage with a laugh. All Gabriel's sheep are killed because of his dog and he is forced to seek employment, finding a place as shepherd with Bathsheba, his love, now a prosperous farmer. Her youngest servant, Fanny Robin, has run away to join her soldier sweetheart. Bathsheba dismisses her bailiff for thieving and deals directly with the other farmers; only Boldwood ignores her. She discusses him with Liddy and idly sends him a valentine. The farmer's attention is drawn and he asks Gabriel to identify Bathsheba's writing.

Who? What? Why? When? Where? How?

1   Levi Everdene, Bathsheba's father (8)
2   Fanny Robin (7)
3   She looks at herself in her mirror; Gabriel concludes that she is vain (1)
4   Her uncle died (8)
5   Because she doesn't love him (4)
6   Because he alone ignores her (12)
7   Outside the cowshed, where she has been milking the cow (3)
8   The malthouse (8)
9   His young dog drives his entire flock of sheep over a precipice. He repays his debts and is left with nothing (5)
10 She tosses him a hymnbook (13)

Who is this?

1   Gabriel (1)
2   Boldwood (12)
3   George, Gabriel's elder dog (5)
4   Liddy (13)
5   Bathsheba (12)
6   Fanny (12)
7   Boldwood – as described by Liddy (9)

Familiar themes

1   Fanny contacts Troy by throwing stones at his window in the barracks wall; the gloom comments upon their doomed relationship, and Fanny's tragedy in particular
2   This is the scene Gabriel observes and remembers as he sees all his flock dead or dying. 'Skeleton' and 'dead' point up the morbid effect and the morning star dogs the moon as Gabriel's dog has his sheep
3   Bathsheba's rick is on fire – the vocabulary stresses light and heat ('red', 'fiery', 'glaring') and unnatural activity ('knots of… worms', "creeping movement')
4   Boldwood's imagination has been caught by the foolish valentine and his obsession with Bathsheba is beginning; the description of the sunrise is oppressive, unnatural in colour – ('garish', 'greenish-yellow') and in design (the sky and earth seem invented)
5   The fresh, bright beauty of Bathsheba as she first appears in the novel is mirrored in the colours of the flowers and the sunshine

Prove it!

1   Bathsheba's aunt speaks to Gabriel about her niece. '…she's so good-looking, and an excellent scholar besides – she was going to be a governess once, you know, only she was too wild.'
2   Billy Smallbury and Joseph Poorgrass are overheard by Gabriel, who is hiding

in the cart. More than one sentence is quotable, but here is an example: 'she's a very vain feymell – so 'tis said here and there.'
3 Bathsheba is discussed generally by her workers in the Malthouse, prompted by Gabriel. An example: 'Tis to be hoped her temper is as good as her face.'
4 Bathsheba is here discussed by the farmers in the cornmarket. 'Yes, 'tis a pity she's so headstrong... But we ought to be proud of her here – she lightens up the old place.'
5 Another scene in the malthouse. Note that Gabriel forbids 'that dalliance-talk' about Bathsheba; Joseph Poorgrass responds: '...'tis a real joyful thing that she's no worse, that's what I say.'

■ Self-test answers Chapters 16–28

Uncover the plot
Boldwood looks properly at Bathsheba and falls in love with her; she is sorry that she sent the valentine. He asks her to marry him in May at the sheep-washing; she at first refuses with dignity but is confused by his vehemence and asks for time to consider. Gabriel criticises her behaviour and she dismisses him angrily, but is forced to beg him to return when her sheep become ill. The shearing takes place in the Great Barn and at the shearing supper, Boldwood proposes again and Bathsheba promises him an answer in a few weeks. That same night, while she looks round the farm before going to bed, her dress becomes entangled in Troy's spur. He gives her his watch and persuades her to come alone to watch him demonstrate his swordplay. He kisses her and she bursts into tears.

Who? What? Why? When? Where? How?
1 Gabriel (18)
2 Troy (27)
3 'It was a fatal omission of Boldwood's that he had never once told her she was beautiful' (24)
4 Bathsheba dismisses him (18)
5 He is watching Boldwood with Bathsheba while he shears (22)
6 He kisses her (28)
7 She, as a farmer, is outside (19)
8 In the Casterbridge Cornmarket, after receiving the valentine (17)
9 She tells him she will try to love him and will give him an answer in five or six weeks (23)
10 They become entangled in the fir plantation, Troy's spur being caught in the hem of Bathsheba's dress (24)

Who is this?
1 Troy (25)
2 Troy (described by Liddy) (24)
3 Troy (26)
4 Bathsheba (21)
5 Boldwood (18)

Parallel lines
1 '...a censor's experience on seeing an actual flirt after observing her would have been a feeling of surprise that Bathsheba could be so different from such a one, and yet so like what a flirt is supposed to be.' (18)
2 Gabriel is really the character in the novel who is exactly as he seems – this is an unusual example '...he inwardly said "I find more bitter than death the woman whose heart is snares and nets!". This was mere exclamation – the froth of the storm. He adored Bathsheba just the same.' (22)

3 'That stillness, which struck casual observers more than anything else in his character and habit, and seemed so precisely like the rest of inanition, may have been the prefect balance of enormous antagonistic forces – positives and negatives in fine adjustment' (18)

4 Virtually any line in this chapter is revealing about Troy! An example: 'He could… be one thing and seem another; for instance, he could speak of love and think of dinner; call on the husband to look at the wife; be eager to pay and intend to owe.' (25)

About time

1 a) Early spring (b) Persuading a ewe to adopt a substitute lamb (c) For example: '…the ground was melodious with ripples, and the sky with larks…' (18)

2 A) End of May (b) Sheep-washing c) For example: 'To the north of the meadow were trees, the leaves of which were new, soft, and moist, not yet having stiffened and darkened under summer sun' (19)

3 a) The first day of June b) Sheep-shearing c) For example: 'Every green was young, every pore was open, and every stalk was swollen with racing currents of juice.' (22)

4 a) Late June b) Hiving the bees c) 'Bathsheba's eyes, shaded by one hand, were following the ascending multitude against the unexplorable stretch of blue till they ultimately halted by one of the unwieldy trees…' (27)

Open quotes

1 '…dignified' (19)

2 'For his bride a soldier sought her,
And a winning tongue had he:
On the banks of the Allan Water
None was gay as she!' (23)

3 '…a firmament of light, and of sharp hisses, resembling a sky-full of meteors close at hand' (28)

4 '…living outside his defences for the first time, and with a fearful sense of exposure.' (18)

5 '…the sound of the trumpet is to silence' (24)

▓ Self-test answers Chapters 29–41

Uncover the plot

Gabriel speaks to Bathsheba about her infatuation with Troy; she breaks off the meeting because she is meeting her lover. She writes to refuse Boldwood – he is violently upset and threatens to harm Troy. She follows Troy to Bath and when she returns, has married him. Troy and Boldwood confront each other and Boldwood is humiliated. On the night of the Harvest Supper, Gabriel worries about a coming storm but Troy dismisses his anxieties and encourages the workers to drink heavily. They all fall asleep. Gabriel alone works to cover the wheatstacks, helped by Bathsheba. Boldwood's ricks are ruined. Bathsheba and Troy quarrel over his gambling and meet Fanny on the road. Troy arranges to bring her money in Casterbridge and she struggles to complete the journey there. News is brought of her death by Joseph Poorgrass and a wagon is sent to fetch her body.

Who? What? Why? When? Where? How?

1 Cain Ball (33)
2 Fanny (40)
3 A lock of Fanny's hair (41)
4 He throws it into the road (34)
5 They are sleeping drunkenly (36)

6 Because he told her 'his constancy could not be relied on unless (she) at once became his…'. She marries him 'between jealousy and distraction.' (37)
7 When she sees the lock of hair in Troy's watch and learns that it was Fanny they met on the road (41)
8 On Yalbury Hill (31)
9 She is helped by a stray dog (40)
10 He shows him the marriage announcement in the paper (34)

Who says this?
1 Gabriel (29)
2 Troy (41)
3 Bathsheba (30)

Who says this, of whom?
1 Cain Ball, describing Bathsheba and Troy (33)
2 Joseph Poorgrass, describing Fanny (41)
3 Fanny, about the stray dog. 'I stoned him away' is the answer (40)
4 Gabriel, about Troy (29)
5 Boldwood (lying, of course) about Bathsheba (38)
6 Jan Coggan, about Boldwood (35)

Prove it!
1 'Bathsheba loved Troy in the way that only self-reliant women love when they abandon their self-reliance. When a strong woman recklessly throws away her strength she is worse than a weak woman who has never had any strength to throw away.' (29)
2 Troy tells Bathsheba that he goes to church secretly through the little gallery door; Gabriel goes to look: 'a sprig of ivy had grown from the wall across the door to a length of more than a foot…' (29)
3 ' "There are considerations even before my consideration for you; reparations to be made – ties you know nothing of." ' (41) (This is spoken to Bathsheba)
4 A tree nearby is struck by lightning: 'A sulphurous smell filled the air; then all was silent… "We had a narrow escape!" said Gabriel hurriedly.' (37)
5 Gabriel discovers that all Boldwood's corn is ruined: ' "I overlooked the ricks this year." ' (38)

■ Self-test answers Chapters 42–57

Uncover the plot
Fanny's coffin is taken to Bathsheba's house overnight and Bathsheba opens it to find out if Fanny had a child. Troy, interrupting her, is full of remorse and kisses the dead mother and child – Bathsheba cries out: 'Kiss me too!'. He repulses her and she runs away, only agreeing to return when Fanny is taken away. Troy buys Fanny a tombstone for £27 and plants flowers on her grave, but rain from a gargoyle destroys his hard work. He leaves in despair and is thought to have drowned. Time passes, and Gabriel becomes bailiff of both farms; Bathsheba agrees to consider marrying Boldwood in 6 years' time. On Christmas Eve, they become engaged but Troy returns and Boldwood shoots him. One rainy day a year later, Bathsheba finally marries Gabriel.

Who? What? Why? When? Where? How?
1 Bathsheba (46)
2 Pennyways, the bailiff (50)
3 Troy seizes Bathsheba's arm and she screams (53)
4 She lays it out in grave-clothes (54)

5   The title is ironic; Fanny is a gentle, unvengeful character, but in her death she gains the ascendancy over Bathsheba by having a child and by being more greatly loved by Troy (43)

6   His clothes are found abandoned on the beach (48)

7   In Gabriel's house, which she has never previously visited (56)

8   In the same grave as Fanny (56)

9   She is not able to speak or move (53)

10   He rubs off the words 'and child' from the coffin lid (42)

Who is this?

1   Bathsheba (54)

2   Fanny (43)

3   Troy (46)

4   Gabriel (as described by Susan Tall) (49)

5   Bathsheba (57)

6   Bathsheba (as described by Laban Tall) (53)

Who are these?

1   Troy and Fanny (described by Bathsheba) (48)

2   Joseph Poorgrass; it comes on when he has had too much to drink and makes him see everything double (42)

3   Gabriel and Bathsheba (58)

4   Troy (to Bathsheba) (43)

Parallel lines

1   Gabriel's dog causes the death of his sheep (5)

2   Bathsheba wears a red coat in Chapter 1 and a red hat helping Gabriel in the storm; the seal on the valentine is red, but, oddly, there is hardly any blood when Troy is shot

3   Troy severs a lock of Bathsheba's hair with his sword (28)

4   'She was indispensable to high generation, hated at tea parties, feared in shops, and loved at crises.' (49)

5   In Chapter 1, Bathsheba is travelling on a wagon laden with furniture and plants to stay with her aunt

6   'On the slope in front of (Gabriel) appeared two human shapes, black as jet. The rick lost its sheen – the shapes vanished… It had been the sixth flash which had come from the east behind him, and the two dark forms on the slope had been the shadows of himself and Bathsheba' (37) The descriptions of the giant shadows are both sinister and awesome – in both cases they indicate that an event of importance is occurring

7   When Bathsheba watches Gabriel shearing (and times him); this 'dim and temperate bliss' is spoilt by Boldwood's appearance b) When they save the ricks from the storm. There are several other descriptions of them working together – for example, in Chapter 18, when they persuade a ewe to adopt a lamb, or at the sheep washing in Chapter 19

8   Twice: He saves her flock from death (21); He saves her ricks from the storm (36 and & 37). Note that Bathsheba saves his life (4); the indebtedness is not all in one direction

9   In Chapter 42, he rubs out the words 'and child' from Fanny's coffin lid. This leads to Bathsheba opening the coffin to find out the truth and from there to the disastrous confrontation with Troy

10   For example: a) Bathsheba's first meeting with Troy b) Boldwood's second proposal of marriage c) Bathsheba takes the horse and tries to go secretly to Bath to meet Troy d) Troy and Boldwood confront each other

Events which occur at night are usually laden with dark and sinister implications; it is noticeable that such scenes increase in number and intensity throughout the novel, until the death of Troy. Compare the early scene in Chapter 2, when Gabriel is described in his hut at night; here, tragic overtones are completely absent